NORSE MYTHOLOGY

NORSE MYTHOLOGY

This edition published in 2023 by Arcturus Publishing Limited
26/27 Bickels Yard, 151–153 Bermondsey Street,
London SE1 3HA

Copyright © Arcturus Holdings Limited

All rights reserved. No part of this publication may be reproduced, stored in a retrieval system, or transmitted, in any form or by any means, electronic, mechanical, photocopying, recording or otherwise, without written permission in accordance with the provisions of the Copyright Act 1956 (as amended). Any person or persons who do any unauthorised act in relation to this publication may be liable to criminal prosecution and civil claims for damages.

Typesetting by Sooky Choi

Cover design: Peter Ridley

AD011675UK

Printed in the UK

CONTENTS

Introduction 9

TALES FROM THE EDDAS

Odin Seeks Wisdom from Mimir – *Litchfield* 15

The Giant Builder – *Brown* 27

How Thiassi Captured Loki – *Litchfield* 36

Thiassi Carries Off Idunn – *Litchfield* 41

The Gods Grow Old – *Litchfield* 46

Loki Brings Back Idunn – *Litchfield* 51

Skadi's Choice – *Brown* 56

Geirröd and Agnar – *Bradish* 62

Freyr – *Bradish* 65

Freyja – *Bradish* 73

Loki and Skyrmsli – *Bradish* 78

Loki Makes Trouble Between the Artists and the
   Gods – *Litchfield* 81

Baldr and Loki – *Litchfield* 89

Baldr's Dreams – *Litchfield* 90

The Mistletoe – *Brown* 95

Thor and Thrym – *Litchfield* 97

Thor and Skrymir – *Litchfield* 103

Thor's Journey to Get the Kettle for Ægir –
Litchfield 121

In the Giant's House – *Brown* 128

Thor's Duel – *Brown* 139

The Binding of the Wolf – *Litchfield* 149

The Death of Baldr – *Litchfield* 154

Baldr's Funeral – *Litchfield* 156

Hermod's Journey in Search of Baldr –
Litchfield 159

Loki at Ægir's Feast – *Litchfield* 163

The Capture of Loki - *Litchfield* 167

The Beginning of Poetry – *Bradish* 170

The Judgment Hall of the Dead – *Bradish* 175

The Twilight of the Gods – *Litchfield* 177

TALES FROM THE SAGAS

The Story of Völund – *Goddard* 182

King Olaf the Saint – *Goddard* 191

King Sigmund – *Bradish* 197

The House of the Helper – *Bradish* 206

Regin's Story – *Bradish* 212

The Forging of the Sword – *Bradish* 220

The Prophecy of the Gripir – *Bradish* 223

The Glittering Heath – *Bradish* 224

Brynhild – *Bradish* 228

Gudrun's Dreams – *Bradish* 232

Sigurd at Lymdale – *Bradish* 237

The Wooing of Brynhild – *Bradish* 241

The Quarrel of the Queens – *Bradish* 247

The End of the Treasure – *Bradish* 254

INTRODUCTION

THE legendary tales of the Norse gods Odin, Thor, Loki and their companions, as they fight amongst each other, battle fierce enemies and meddle with troublesome humans, are some of the most entertaining and fascinating stories of all mythology. Their names remain with us in the days of the week: for example, Wednesday is 'Wodan's Day' (Wodan being an alternative name for Odin). The myths and legends of the Norsemen were shared by all the Germanic peoples of Europe, and provided a unique alternative to the two competing cultures of the continent in the early centuries CE – the increasingly powerful and prescriptive Christianity, and the slowly fading, if widely known, tales of Greek and Roman mythology.

The old stories of the men and women of Scandinavia have been retold countless times and inspired many works of fiction. Fantasy and science fiction owe much to Norse mythology, with its characters, creatures and deities worming their way, in altered forms, into J R R Tolkien's *Lord of the Rings* and Neil Gaiman's *American Gods*. In music, Norse mythology has inspired as diverse creations as Richard Wagner's *Ring Cycle* and modern heavy metal. While the names of Mjöllnir, Asgard, the Valkyries and Ragnarök have crept into modern usage.

The tales found their first written expression in two Icelandic 'Eddas'. The elder of the two is known as the *Poetic Edda* and derives from the medieval manuscript of the *Codex Regius*, often attributed to the twelfth-century priest Saemund. The younger collection is the *Prose Edda*, written by Snorri Sturluson in the early thirteenth century. It is from these two sources that almost all knowledge of the Norse mythological world derives.

The gods of the Norsemen were strangely complicated. Like the Greek inhabitants of Mount Olympus, they were often selfish, petty and quick to anger, but they could also display great generosity and were prepared for immense sacrifice. Thor, with his trusty hammer Mjöllnir, held immense power, but could easily be tricked; Loki was the trickster, but he was far more than the mere personification of evil; the one-eyed Odin was a wise and cunning deity locked in pursuit of knowledge. In short, the gods were not so different from men.

In Norse cosmology, the world began after Ymir, the first giant, was formed from the meeting of the frost of Niflheim and the flames of Muspelheim. The cow Audhumbla uncovered a group of gods known as the Æsir that included Odin, who slew Ymir and created the earth from his corpse. The Ash Tree of Life, Yggdrasil, sat at the centre of the Nine Worlds. The gods resided in the upper world of Asgard while humanity dwelt in the central world of Midgard. Mary Litchfield explained more about this in the Introductory Chapter (see page 16).

Through these worlds were found creatures such as elves, dwarves and frost giants. In death, men might be condemned to Hel; be carried away by the Valkyries to Valhalla, a heavenly feasting hall reserved for the brave who died in combat; or chosen by Freyja to dwell in the field of Folkvangr. In Valhalla, the martial heroes of Midgard joined Thor in preparation for Ragnarök. Also known as 'The Twilight of the Gods', Ragnarök consisted of a great battle between the gods and the frost giants, culminating in the destruction of the world before its eventual rebirth.

War beset the divine world just as it did the mortal one. The Norse gods divided into two tribes – the Æsir and the Vanir, who were often at odds with each other. Gods, such as Thor, Heimdall and Frigg, belonged to the Æsir, with Odin as their leader. The Vanir included Njörd and his children Freyr and Freyja, amongst others. The Æsir were known for their warlike qualities and the Vanir for fertility and wisdom.

In the myths collected here, we discover how the world began and how Odin lost his eye. We follow Loki's adventures, his courting of Idunn and his troublemaking, to the cost of the beloved god Baldr. We learn of Thor's adventures and his efforts to recover the famous hammer Mjöllnir. We hear of Freyr and Freyja, of the great wolf Fenris, of the Æsir–Vanir war and of the origin of poetry. And of course, we learn of Ragnarök, the Twilight of the Gods.

The fabulous tales of the Viking world do not end with the occurrences in Asgard. Unlike early literary accounts from many other cultures, the storytelling tradition of the Eddas found its way into the recording of history. For centuries, the men of the North recounted the tales of their heroes, their kings and their great adventures in the Sagas. The story of Sigurd, recorded in the 'Völsunga Saga', has everything to recommend it – power struggles, a battle with a dragon, heartwarming romance, a cursed ring and even moral lessons to take away.

Like the fairy-tales of medieval Europe, the legends are often infused with moral lessons. They explain to men and women how they should behave but they are also used to provide a sense of history. It is from the Sagas that we derive most of our knowledge of Scandinavian and Icelandic history in the era before Christianity took hold. Sometimes literal, sometimes allegorical, they are both entertaining and powerful reminders of a half-forgotten world.

For centuries, the stories of the Norsemen vanished into obscurity. In the late nineteenth century, however, a determined effort was made to restore them to public view. This was largely thanks to the work of writers like Mary Litchfield, Sarah Bradish, Edward Ernest Kellett and William Morris – whose interpretations and translations are included in this collection, in all their variety of writing styles and viewpoints, sometimes overlapping or contradicting but ultimately combining to create a charismatic picture of a world both familiar and mysterious. As evidenced by its influence in so many fields of literature and creativity today, Norse mythology has, deservedly, never been more popular.

TALES FROM THE EDDAS

ODIN SEEKS WISDOM FROM MIMIR

as told by Mary Litchfield

It was night in Asgard, the home of the gods. A soft light fell upon the sleeping city, showing its vine-clad hills and glittering palaces, and touching even the deep, still valleys that lay between. For the trembling bridge, Bifröst, spanned the city like a rainbow of silver, meeting the horizon at the north and south. Toward the south, as far as the eye could reach, rose mountains, with castles upon their tops and sides; while toward the north stretched the level and grassy plains of Ida.

From a structure upon the highest place of the city, a shaft shot up, slender and glittering, as a tall spire rises from some great cathedral. It rose high above all the castles and towers, so high as almost to touch the arch of the celestial bridge. This slender shaft was Odin's High Seat. From its top could be seen not only Asgard, but also a large part of the worlds below.

Here the Allfather sat alone, buried in thought. Alone except for two wolves that lay sleeping at his feet, and two ravens[1] perched upon his shoulders, weary after their journey through the nine worlds.

---

1. Odin's ravens were Hugin (thought) and Munin (memory); each day they flew over the nine worlds, bringing back tidings to Odin.

After sitting a long while in meditation, Odin looked down upon the stately homes of his children, and upon the fields that stretched away, beyond the high walls and the dark, rushing river that surrounded the city of the gods. Then his eyes tried in vain to pierce the dense blackness that shrouded a land far below him toward the north. He gazed long and earnestly, and at last rose up and descended quickly to the palace just below his High Seat. The vast halls resounded as he strode through them.

He hastened to a building nearby, and soon appeared again, leading a grey horse. This horse was well fitted to bear the father of the gods; for he had a powerful frame and eight legs. As he stood waiting for Odin to mount, he trembled with eagerness, and flames poured from his nostrils. In an instant Odin was on his back, and the wonderful horse was carrying him toward the north with the speed of the wind.

The high wall and the dark river surrounding the city were no obstacle to Sleipnir. He leaped easily over them, and kept on his swift way across the fields on the other side, which stretched green and level to the distant horizon. Here and there were groves in whose quiet depths a less rapid traveller might have heard the trickling of fountains. And occasionally a lake reflected on its dark surface the silvery arch of Bifröst.

At last they reached the point where the celestial bridge touched the outer edge of Asgard. The eight-footed horse rushed unhesitatingly upon the bridge, although it trembled beneath his weight, sending up fitful flames. Like a comet among the stars, Sleipnir sped on, bearing Odin over the black depths.

At length a faint light reached them from the north; and soon Odin saw a horseman, clad in a white garment, coming towards him. The horse had a mane of gold, which, shining full upon the rider, revealed his pure, pale face. Approaching, he said, 'Welcome, Father Odin. I have been watching for you ever since I heard Sleipnir's eight hoofs strike the bridge. Doubtless some deep purpose brings you across Bifröst at night?'

'Yes, Heimdall, you have judged rightly,' said Odin; 'a great matter urges me on; and many days must I journey ere I return home. I must go through the dark land of our enemies, the frost giants of the lower world; and then far beyond, to regions that few have visited. Fortunate are the gods that Heimdall guards for them the trembling bridge. Were it not for your keen ears that hear the grass growing and the wool thickening on the backs of the sheep, our enemies might, ere this, have crossed the abyss, and have stormed Asgard.'

As he spoke, they both looked down upon the land beneath them, dark, except for the light that streamed from Heimdall's far-shining castle at the bridge-head. And they could see the glistening tops of ice mountains rising above the mists.

As Odin looked he said, 'Our enemies are strong, and I fear the treacherous Loki, who is ever going between Asgard and the giant-world. We have need of all your watchfulness, Heimdall, and of all the strength of Thor, the dread foe of the giants, to keep our enemies at bay. What great wisdom do I need to protect the realm of Asgard, and the world of men!'

They kept on their way toward Heimdall's castle, which was on a high mountain near the bridge-head. The castle was apparently made of the same material as the bridge, and, as it rose toward the sky, might have been taken for a structure of cloud bathed in moonlight. But in truth it shone with a soft fire of its own; for radiance streamed from it in all directions, lighting up, as we have seen, a part of the cold, foggy land of the giants. The approach to the bridge was in this way made so clearly visible that it would have been impossible for anyone to get near without Heimdall's knowledge, even had his hearing been less keen. Then, too, the castle was strongly fortified, surrounded by a high wall and a moat, the waters of which, like those of the Asgard river, were covered with a mist that flashed into flames when disturbed by an enemy of the gods.

'Come in, Odin,' said Heimdall, as they reached the castle; 'your journey has been long, and a hard road lies before you.'

They entered a large hall whose walls were made of something that resembled white marble or alabaster. All the decorations were of silver. Vines bearing clusters of silver grapes ran along the walls, and curious horns and lamps hung from the arches above. Tall youths, clad, like Heimdall, all in white, brought in tankards of foaming mead.[2]

The two gods drank the mead, and talked earnestly together, until at last Odin rose, saying, 'One favour I ask of you, Heimdall: keep Sleipnir for me until my return. There are few to whom I would entrust him, but he will be safe with you. I wish to journey, unknown, through the world of cold and darkness, and the horse would betray me.'

Heimdall accompanied Odin a short distance down the steep mountain, and then returned to his post, to guard the bridge of the gods.

---

2. Honey and water, fermented and flavoured.

3. The giant-world in the northern part of the great under-world.

As Odin went down into Niflheim,[3] a chilly fog closed about him, shutting out the light from Heimdall's castle, and making it hard for him to keep to the path. As he got lower, the cold became intense, and his foot slipped on the icy road which broadened into a river of ice. There were sounds of creaking and crashing, and in the distance could be heard the moaning of waves as they broke upon the desolate shore. As he made his way he could just distinguish through the mist and darkness the enormous mountains of ice surrounding him. Some of these seeming ice mountains were really frost giants whose huge heads would slowly turn to follow him. Once an iceberg in the sea went to pieces with the noise of distant thunder, and he could long hear the booming and crashing. Sometimes a deluge of icy water would rush upon him from a cascade that he had not perceived; and then he would hear the slow, heavy laughter of the giants, sounding like the roar of hoarse winds. At one point in his journey he came upon a field of ice; and as the fog lifted, he could see that it stretched on all sides, level and white, covered with snow. Here the sounds of creaking and crashing ceased, and he no longer heard the laughter of the giants: the silence was absolute. He stood alone under the stars.

After a long journey through the ice region, Odin reached a country where dark, savage mountains took the place of icebergs, and here and there on their peaks loomed up the strongholds of the mountain giants. As he kept on his way, he could sometimes distinguish the giants themselves, looking like huge, moving masses of rock. This land was as dreary as the land of ice; for although there was no fog, and a faint twilight glimmered, it was very desolate. Not a green thing was to be seen; nothing but grim mountains and dark abysses, at the bottom of which rushed rivers, finding their way from the spring Hvergelmir to the cold northern sea. The mountains, at times, gave place to level wastes of great extent, where boulders lay heaped one upon another, with deep, still pools lurking among them. Often heavy clouds rolled across the sky, enveloping the mountains.

After journeying long, Odin stood upon a high place from which he could look down upon a morass stretching as far as the eye could reach. In the dim light he could just distinguish a narrow footpath of solid ground leading across it. When he was partly over, one of the giants saw him; and soon a troop of the monsters came stumbling after him. Finding it impossible to reach him, they filled the air with their shouts, and brandished their great clubs. Upon this a fearful wind arose, threatening to blow Odin from the narrow path. Clouds shaped like dragons blew gusts at him from their open mouths; and when he got safely over, howls of disappointed rage resounded long in the air behind.

He came next to a river, whose dark, swift current bore with it sharp stones and bits of iron, and no bridge spanned the deadly stream; but Odin crossed it safely on some driftwood.

Higher mountains than any he had yet seen now loomed up toward the south; and one, higher than the others, down whose sides rushed twelve rivers. On the top of this mountain was the ice-cold spring Hvergelmir. One of the three roots of the great World Tree, Yggdrasil, was bathed by the waters of this spring; and the rivers that flowed from it went in all directions; some flowing through the cold, foggy land of the giants to the northern ocean, while others flowed toward the south, through the vast realms where Mimir[4] and Urd[5] guarded their wells under the other two roots of the World Tree.

As Odin neared the mountain, his way led through a gloomy cave, where he could hear the baying of a dog and the creaking of an iron gate. This gate, he knew, barred the descent to the world of torture below Niflheim – a world far more dark and dreadful than that through which he had just passed. Once out of the cave, the road led over the mountain. On the highest peak stood a solitary watchman, the trusty guardian of the spring and the dread foe of the giants.

As Odin came near, he greeted him: 'Did the monsters try to harm you, Odin? The hateful crew would be glad enough to crush the father of the gods and get possession of Asgard. And your Loki is too much with them. I often see him there. He thinks himself well hidden by the darkness; but my eyes are trained to see in the dark.'

'Yes, Egil,' replied Odin; 'your eyes and Heimdall's ears are the best defence we have against our foes. I came through safely, as you see. Their attacks would have been more fierce had they known me. As for Loki, I am well aware how dangerous he has become. Still, I may not yet turn him out of Asgard, for I am bound by an oath made when we both were young – when I thought him innocent. But I must hasten, Egil; a great purpose urges me on.'

As Odin went down the southern slope of the mountain, a pleasant prospect greeted his eyes, wearied with the gloomy sights upon which they had been looking for so many days. The country was still mountainous, but it was not black and sterile. Rich metals

---

4. The giant who grew from under Ymir's arm.

5. Urd and her two sisters were Norns, or Fates, representing the past, present and future.

seamed the rocks, and here and there were the mouths of caves where sparkled crystals and gems. When Odin stopped and listened, he could hear the picks and hammers of the dwarfs. Twilight still hung over the scene, but at intervals lights streamed across the sky, their rich colours playing upon the mountains.

Odin had now to cross a broad river, and then he could see in the distance a castle of fantastic shape, which was ornamented in an unusual manner. Stone dragons grinned from its corners, their large jewelled eyes gleaming like fire as the lights flashed upon them. About the slender columns twined golden snakes and lizards of copper; and metal vines ran thickly along the walls, bearing gems for flowers. A fire shone from one part of the building, and it was evident that work of some kind was going on.

This strange castle was the home of Sindri and his brothers – dwarfs and famous artists, who had made wonderful weapons and ornaments for the gods. None approached them in skill except the sons of Ivaldi. The latter were partly of giant blood, and were said to be magicians as well as artists. Between them and the dwarfs there was some rivalry, but, as yet, no hard feeling. Odin passed near the castle, but did not enter.

As he went on, the mountains lost all their savage wildness, and rose in gentle outlines against the sky. They were clothed with forests and vineyards. Down their slopes rushed brooks, changing into cascades of mist. Peaceful valleys stretched between the mountains; while high above all were clouds, glowing with the colours of an eternal sunset. For this was a land where dark night and glaring midday never came.

The mountains gradually softened into hills, and these, at last, were lost in broad stretches of level fields covered with golden grain or tall, waving grass. The rivers glided along, deep and peaceful. Flowers bloomed everywhere, their bright colours reflected in the still waters of little ponds. Herds of deer came timidly up to Odin, and birds sang to him as he passed. Only the gentlest breeze stirred the leaves, and all sounds were low and sweet.

Along the southern horizon there now appeared a bank of white clouds, piled high, one upon another. But as Odin neared them, they changed to mountains of marble, evidently enclosing some sacred spot. Like pure white sentinels they stood, bathed with rich colours.

There seemed to be no entrance through this marble wall; but when Odin reached it, he knocked with his staff, and a door was opened. A man of grave and reverend aspect greeted him, and led the way through a spacious cave sparkling with crystals that reflected the light of his torch. At the further end of the cave was a door, larger than the one by which Odin had entered, opening into a circular valley.

The sides of the valley were formed by the marble mountains; but they did not look like mountains on the inside; for they had been carved into beautiful shapes, and delicate vines ran over them, veiling the whiteness of the marble.

From the centre of the valley grew the root of the enormous World Tree; and the waters of the deep well of wisdom bathed the root of the tree. At the further end of the valley rose a stately palace. Here and there were groups of trees, and rare plants bloomed on all sides. Near a pool a large turtle, his back covered with the incrustations of ages, basked lazily in the light. Harmless serpents with brilliant eyes twined about the trunks of trees. Dragons slept with folded wings, while many ancient and uncouth monsters rested amid the groves, or sunned themselves in the niches of the marble walls. Gay-coloured birds flitted in and out among the branches, and peacocks walked proudly about, spreading their tails. The scene was made more fair by the light that fell upon it. It was not sunlight, and one could not tell whence it came; but it flooded the peaceful valley with the softest radiance.

Odin stood for a few moments looking at the scene before him, and then walked slowly toward the centre of the valley. Under the root of the World Tree sat a man of giant stature, apparently absorbed in watching the waters of the well. Long silver locks floated over his shoulders, and a white beard fell upon his breast. There was no look of old age in his face, although, as he raised his head, the wisdom of the centuries gleamed from his deep blue eyes, and his whole aspect expressed perfect peace. His hand rested upon the edge of the well, which was thickly overlaid with gold. Near him stood an immense chest, curiously carved, containing treasures from bygone ages. A large horn of silver lay upon the chest, bearing Heimdair's name in runic characters of gold.

As Odin came near, Mimir rose, saying, 'Welcome, Odin! You come from the north, I see. This time you have chosen the hard road, and on foot too!'

'Yes, Mimir,' answered Odin; 'I chose that road because I wished to explore the land of my enemies, and I have come to you for counsel and help.'

'Gladly will I help you, as you know,' said Mimir.

'I know your readiness,' replied Odin; 'but this time I ask what no one has ever asked of you. My realm is beset with dangers. Loki grows in wickedness. He has taken for his wife the witch of the iron-wood, and their children threaten to prove our most formidable foes. And the frost giants and the mountain giants, as you know, are only too ready to attack us whenever there is a chance of success. I need great wisdom rightly to govern and protect Asgard, and Midgard, the world of men.'

Both were silent for a moment; and then Odin said, looking earnestly at Mimir, 'In order that I may gain this wisdom, I ask for one drink from your deep well.'

After a long silence, Mimir said slowly, 'You have asked a great thing, Odin! Are you prepared to pay the price for it?'

'Yes,' replied Odin, eagerly; 'all the gold of Asgard, our best swords, our jewelled shields! Even Sleipnir will I give you for one draught of the precious water!'

'These things will not buy what you desire,' said Mimir; 'wisdom can be gained only by suffering and sacrifice. Would you give one of your eyes for wisdom?'

A cloud came over the bold face of Odin, and he pondered long. Finally he said slowly, 'I will give one of my eyes, and I will suffer whatever else is necessary, if I may thereby gain the wisdom I need.'

No one ever knew all that Odin suffered and learned in that mysterious valley. Some say that he really gave one of his eyes in return for the drink from Mimir's well. But as nothing is said of that in the old song called 'Odin's Rune Song', and as the fact of his being one-eyed is not mentioned in some of the oldest poems, it seems doubtful whether that sacrifice was required of him. Odin says in his 'Rune Song':

> I know that I hung
> on a wind-rocked tree,
> nine whole nights,
> with a spear wounded
> and to Odin offered,

myself to myself;
on that tree,
of which no one knows
from what root it springs.

Bread no one gave me,
nor a horn of drink;
downward I peered,
to runes applied myself,
wailing learnt them,
then fell down thence.

Potent songs nine
from the famed son,
I learned, of Bolthorn, Bestla's sire,
and a draught obtained
of the precious mead
drawn from Odhraerir.

Then I began to bear fruit,
and to know many things,
to grow and well thrive:
word by word
I sought out words,
fact by fact
I sought out facts.[6]

---

6. From 'Odin's Rune Song' in Thorpe's translation of *Saemund's Edda*.

THE GIANT BUILDER

as told by Abbie Farewell Brown

Ages and ages ago, when the world was first made, the gods decided to build a beautiful city high above the heavens, the most glorious and wonderful city that ever was known. Asgard was to be its name, and it was to stand on Ida Plain under the shade of Yggdrasil, the great tree whose roots were underneath the earth.

First of all they built a house with a silver roof, where there were seats for all the twelve chiefs. In the midst, and high above the rest, was the wonder-throne of Odin the All-Father, whence he could see everything that happened in the sky or on the earth or in the sea. Next they made a fair house for Queen Frigg and her lovely daughters. Then they built a smithy, with its great hammers, tongs, anvils and bellows, where the gods could work at their favourite trade, the making of beautiful things out of gold; which they did so well that folk name that time the Golden Age. Afterwards, as they had more leisure, they built separate houses for all the Æsir, each more beautiful than the preceding, for of course they were continually growing more skilful. They saved Father Odin's palace until the last, for they meant this to be the largest and the most splendid of all.

Gladsheim, the home of joy, was the name of Odin's house, and it was built all of gold, set in the midst of a wood whereof the trees had leaves of ruddy gold – like an autumn-gilded forest. For the safety of All-Father it was surrounded by a roaring river and by a high picket fence; and there was a great courtyard within.

The glory of Gladsheim was its wondrous hall, radiant with gold, the most lovely room that time has ever seen. Valhalla, the Hall of Heroes, was the name of it, and it was roofed with the mighty shields of warriors. The ceiling was made of interlacing spears, and there was a portal at the west end before which hung a great grey wolf, while over him a fierce eagle hovered. The hall was so huge that it had 540 gates, through each of which 800 men could march abreast. Indeed, there needed to be room, for this was the hall where every morning Odin received all the brave warriors who had died in battle on the earth below; and there were many heroes in those days.

This was the reward which the gods gave to courage. When a hero had gloriously lost his life, the Valkyries, the nine warrior daughters of Odin, brought his body up to Valhalla on their white horses that gallop the clouds. There they lived forever after in happiness, enjoying the things that they had most loved upon earth. Every morning they armed themselves and went out to fight with one another in the great courtyard. It was a wondrous game, wondrously played. No matter how often a hero was killed, he became alive again in time to return perfectly well to Valhalla, where he ate a delicious breakfast with the Æsir; while the beautiful Valkyries who had first brought him thither waited at table and poured the blessed mead, which only the immortal taste. A happy life it was for the heroes, and a happy life for all who dwelt in Asgard; for this was before trouble had come among the gods, following the mischief of Loki.

This is how the trouble began. From the beginning of time, the giants had been unfriendly to the Æsir, because the giants were older and huger and more wicked; besides, they were jealous because the good Æsir were fast gaining more wisdom and power than the giants had ever known. It was the Æsir who set the fair brother and sister, Sun and Moon, in the sky to give light to men; and it was they also who made the jewelled stars out of sparks from the place of fire. The giants hated the Æsir, and tried all in their power to injure them and the men of the earth below, whom the Æsir loved and cared for. The gods had already built a wall around Midgard, the world of men, to keep the giants out; built it of the bushy eyebrows of Ymir, the oldest and hugest of giants. Between Asgard and the giants flowed Ifing, the great river on which ice never formed, and which the gods crossed on the rainbow bridge. But this was not protection enough. Their beautiful new city needed a fortress.

So the word went forth in Asgard, 'We must build us a fortress against the giants; the hugest, strongest, finest fortress that ever was built.'

Now one day, soon after they had announced this decision, there came a mighty man stalking up the rainbow bridge that led to Asgard city.

'Who goes there?' cried Heimdal the watchman, whose eyes were so keen that he could see for a hundred miles around, and whose ears were so sharp that he could hear the grass growing in the meadow and the wool on the backs of the sheep. 'Who goes there? No one can enter Asgard if I say no.'

'I am a builder,' said the stranger, who was a huge fellow with sleeves rolled up to show the iron muscles of his arms. 'I am a builder of strong towers, and I have heard that the folk of Asgard need one to help them raise a fair fortress in their city.'

Heimdal looked at the stranger narrowly, for there was that about him which his sharp eyes did not like. But he made no answer, only blew on his golden horn, which was so loud that it sounded through all the world. At this signal all the Æsir came running to the rainbow bridge, from wherever they happened to be, to find out who was coming to Asgard. For it was Heimdal's duty ever to warn them of the approach of the unknown.

'This fellow says he is a builder,' quoth Heimdal. 'And he would fain build us a fortress in the city.'

'Ay, that I would,' nodded the stranger. 'Look at my iron arm; look at my broad back; look at my shoulders. Am I not the workman you need?'

'Truly, he is a mighty figure,' vowed Odin, looking at him approvingly. 'How long will it take you alone to build our fortress? We can allow but one stranger at a time within our city, for safety's sake.'

'In three half-years,' replied the stranger, 'I will undertake to build for you a castle so strong that not even the giants, should they swarm hither over Midgard – not even they could enter without your leave.'

'Aha!' cried Father Odin, well pleased at this offer. 'And what reward do you ask, friend, for help so timely?'

The stranger hummed and hawed and pulled his long beard while he thought. Then he spoke suddenly, as if the idea had just come into his mind. 'I will name my price, friends,' he said; 'a small price for so great a deed. I ask you to give me Freyja for my wife, and those two sparkling jewels, the Sun and Moon.'

At this demand the gods looked grave; for Freyja was their dearest treasure. She was the most beautiful maid who ever lived, the light and life of heaven, and if she should leave Asgard, joy would go with her; while the Sun and Moon were the light and life of the Æsir's children, men, who lived in the little world below. But Loki the sly whispered that they would be safe enough if they made another condition on their part, so hard that the builder could not fulfil it. After thinking cautiously, he spoke for them all.

'Mighty man,' quoth he, 'we are willing to agree to your price – upon one condition. It is too long a time that you ask; we cannot wait three half-years for our castle; that is equal to three centuries when one is in a hurry. See that you finish the fort without help in one winter, one short winter, and you shall have fair Freyja with the Sun and Moon. But if, on the first day of summer, one stone is wanting to the walls, or if anyone has given you aid in the building, then your reward is lost, and you shall depart without payment.' So spoke Loki, in the name of all the gods; but the plan was his own.

At first the stranger shook his head and frowned, saying that in so short a time no one unaided could complete the undertaking. At last he made another offer. 'Let me have but my good horse to help me, and I will try,' he urged. 'Let me bring the useful Svadilföri with me to the task, and I will finish the work in one winter of short days, or lose my reward. Surely, you will not deny me this little help, from one four-footed friend.'

Then again the Æsir consulted, and the wiser of them were doubtful whether it were best to accept the stranger's offer so strangely made. But again Loki urged them to accept. 'Surely, there is no harm,' he said. 'Even with his old horse to help him, he cannot build the castle in the promised time. We shall gain a fortress without trouble and with never a price to pay.'

Loki was so eager that, although the other Æsir did not like this crafty way of making bargains, they finally consented. Then in the presence of the heroes, with the Valkyries and Mimer's head for witnesses, the stranger and the Æsir gave solemn promise that the bargain should be kept.

On the first day of winter the strange builder began his work, and wondrous was the way he set about it. His strength seemed as the strength of a hundred men. As for his horse Svadilföri, he did more work by half than even the mighty builder. In the night he dragged the enormous rocks that were to be used in building the castle, rocks as big as mountains of the earth; while in the daytime the stranger piled them into place with his iron arms. The Æsir watched him with amazement; never was seen such strength in Asgard. Neither Tyr the stout nor Thor the strong could match the power of the stranger. The gods began to look at one another uneasily. Who was this mighty one who had come among them, and what if after all he should win his reward? Freyja trembled in her palace, and the Sun and Moon grew dim with fear.

Still the work went on, and the fort was piling higher and higher, by day and by night. There were but three days left before the end of winter, and already the building was so tall and so strong that it was safe from the attacks of any giant. The Æsir were delighted with their fine new castle; but their pride was dimmed by the fear that it must be paid for at all too costly a price. For only the gateway remained to be completed, and unless the stranger should fail to finish that in the next three days, they must give him Freyja with the Sun and Moon.

The Æsir held a meeting upon Ida Plain, a meeting full of fear and anger. At last they realized what they had done; they had made a bargain with one of the giants, their enemies; and if he won the prize, it would mean sorrow and darkness in heaven and upon earth. 'How did we happen to agree to so mad a bargain?' they asked one another. 'Who suggested the wicked plan which bids fair to cost us all that we most cherish?' Then they remembered that it was Loki who had made the plan; it was he who had insisted that it be carried out and they blamed him for all the trouble.

'It is your counsels, Loki, that have brought this danger upon us,' quoth Father Odin, frowning. 'You chose the way of guile, which is not our way. It now remains for you to help us by guile, if you can. But if you cannot save for us Freyja and the Sun and Moon, you shall die. This is my word.' All the other Æsir agreed that this was just. Thor alone was away hunting evil demons at the other end of the world, so he did not know what was going on, and what dangers were threatening Asgard.

Loki was much frightened at the word of All-Father. 'It was my fault,' he cried, 'but how was I to know that he was a giant? He had disguised himself so that he seemed but a strong man. And as for his horse – it looks much like that of other folk. If it were not for the horse, he could not finish the work. Ha! I have a thought! The builder shall not finish the gate; the giant shall not receive his payment. I will cheat the fellow.'

Now it was the last night of winter, and there remained but a few stones to put in place on the top of the wondrous gateway. The giant was sure of his prize, and chuckled to himself as he went out with his horse to drag the remaining stones; for he did not know that the Æsir had guessed at last who he was, and that Loki was plotting to outwit him. Hardly had he gone to work when out of the wood came running a pretty little mare, who neighed to Svadilföri as if inviting the tired horse to leave his work and come to the green fields for a holiday.

Svadilföri, you must remember, had been working hard all winter, with never a sight of a four-footed creature of his kind, and he was very lonesome and tired of dragging stones. Giving a snort of disobedience, off he ran after this new friend towards the grassy meadows. Off went the giant after him, howling with rage, and running for dear life, as he saw not only his horse but his chance of success slipping out of reach. It was a mad chase, and all Asgard thundered with the noise of galloping hoofs and the giant's mighty tread. The mare who raced ahead was Loki in disguise, and he led Svadilföri far out of reach, to a hidden meadow that he knew; so that the giant howled and panted up and down all night long, without catching even a sight of his horse.

Now when the morning came the gateway was still unfinished, and night and winter had ended at the same hour. The giant's time was over, and he had forfeited his reward. The Æsir came flocking to the gateway, and how they laughed and triumphed when they found three stones wanting to complete the gate!

'You have failed, fellow,' judged Father Odin sternly, 'and no price shall we pay for work that is still undone. You have failed. Leave Asgard quickly; we have seen all we want of you and of your race.'

Then the giant knew that he was discovered, and he was mad with rage. 'It was a trick!' he bellowed, assuming his own proper form, which was huge as a mountain, and towered high beside the fortress that he had built. 'It was a wicked trick. You shall pay for this in one way or another. I cannot tear down the castle which, ungrateful ones, I have built you, stronger than the strength of any giant. But I will demolish the rest of your shining city!' Indeed, he would have done so in his mighty rage; but at this moment Thor, whom Heimdal had called from the end of the earth by one blast of the golden horn, came rushing to the rescue, drawn in his chariot of goats. Thor jumped to the ground close beside the giant, and before that huge fellow knew what had happened, his head was rolling upon the ground at Father Odin's feet; for with one blow Thor had put an end to the giant's wickedness and had saved Asgard.

'This is the reward you deserve!' Thor cried. 'Not Freyja nor the Sun and Moon, but the death that I have in store for all the enemies of the Æsir.'

In this extraordinary way the noble city of Asgard was made safe and complete by the addition of a fortress which no one, not even the giant who built it, could injure, it was so wonder-strong. But always at the top of the gate were lacking three great stones that no one was mighty enough to lift. This was a reminder to the Æsir that now they had the race of giants for their everlasting enemies. And though Loki's trick had saved them Freyja, and for the world the Sun and Moon, it was the beginning of trouble in Asgard which lasted as long as Loki lived to make mischief with his guile.

HOW THIASSI CAPTURED LOKI

as told by Mary Litchfield

Odin, Loki and another god set out upon a journey. The road lay through thickets, where they could scarcely make their way, and up steep hills; so that fatigue and hunger at last compelled them to stop. They threw themselves down on the edge of a field where some oxen and cows were grazing. Loki, whose appetite was always keen, suggested that one of the oxen would make a good meal. In a few moments the creature was captured and killed. While Loki was preparing the meat for boiling, the other gods brought boughs and small trees to make the fire. Then they retired into the shade.

Loki watched the fire with delight. The red flames sent their forked tongues up around the huge iron kettle, the steam rose in clouds, and the water hissed as the pot boiled over. He laughed gleefully, and cried, 'Burn, fire, hot and high, and cook us a dinner fit for gods!' And he threw on more wood.

Soon it was time for the meat to be done. So Loki found a forked stick and fished out a piece, which he examined and tasted. To his astonishment, it was as raw as when first put in. He stared at the pot, and at the fire, with a look of bewilderment. Then he piled on wood till the fire roared.

In a little while he again tried the meat, but with no better success: it was still raw. The fooler of others, the knave among the gods, was at his wits' end. He gazed at the kettle, exclaiming, 'The evil powers are at work! The frost giants have got into the fire!'

Just then he heard a mocking laugh, which seemed to come from above. And looking up, he saw an enormous eagle that returned his gaze with a steady stare that nearly put him out of countenance; for the eagle's eyes shone like stars.

Finally the bird spoke: 'Well, friend Loki, why doesn't your meat cook? You seem to lack skill, or else bad luck attends you. Give me my share of the feast, and the meat will be done soon enough.'

Loki was already out of patience, and the words of the eagle made him angry. 'Stop your jeering,' he cried, 'or you shall feel the might of an Asa!'

Then the mocking laugh sounded again; and the eagle said, 'Keep your threats, Loki, for those whom you can reach. You are 'little pot, soon hot', unlike your big kettle there.'

The god was now thoroughly enraged; but knowing himself to be helpless, he controlled his anger, and said mildly, 'Suppose we stop our jesting and get the meat cooked. Take your portion, if it will help matters. The meat is bewitched.'

Upon this, the eagle swooped down, and seizing a leg and two shoulders of the ox – which might certainly be called the lion's share – was about to fly off with them, when Loki, seeing what he had done, quickly seized a long pole that was lying near, and struck him a hard blow. But, alas for Loki! The pole stuck fast to the eagle's back, and the other end would not leave Loki's hands. The bird sailed up into the air, carrying with him the astonished god. He soon lowered his flight, so that Loki was dragged over trees and sharp rocks till he howled with pain.

After a while the eagle, tired from carrying so heavy a burden, stopped on the crest of a hill and looked around at his captive. The latter was nearly dead with fright and pain; but he got his breath in a moment, and began to beg for mercy.

The bird listened to him, and laughed his mocking laugh again, as he said, 'Don't you know me yet, Loki? Do you forget your friends so soon?'

Loki stared for a moment, and then cried, 'You are Thiassi!'

'Of course I am Thiassi,' replied the bird. 'I did not think you could be so easily deceived. But I have no desire to harm you. It is the other gods I wish to reach – those who pronounced in favour of the dwarfs.

'Dearly shall they pay for the insult done to us! They shall yet feel the edge of the fatal sword!' And the eagle's eyes flashed.

'How can I serve you?' said Loki. 'Do not count me an enemy, I beg of you.'

'I know you of old, Loki,' replied Thiassi; 'and I know that mischief delights you whether the victim be friend or foe. The game I am going to play will be after your own heart. Idunn,[7] as you may remember, is a kinswoman of mine. I saw her the day the judgment was pronounced – the first time in years. I fancy she must at times weary of the charming monotony of Asgard, and long for a peep at her giant kin. I intend to gratify her unspoken wish. In so doing I shall cause some discomfort to my enemies, the fair gods. Their brows will soon be wrinkled and their forms bent, if the charming Idunn, with her golden apples, leaves them.'

At the picture of the happy gods careworn and wrinkled, Loki laughed aloud, forgetting his recent pain. 'Thiassi, your plan is excellent, and I will help you carry it out!' he cried. 'But in return

---

7. Idun or Idunn, usual form, sometimes Anglicized as Iduna; the goddess of early spring.

promise to do one thing for me. It will hurt your foes more than the loss of Idunn.'

'Speak,' said Thiassi. 'I will do anything for revenge.'

'To injure the gods most deeply,' said Loki, 'one must hurt Baldr. He is their idol. They worship him, as though he were a higher kind of being – even Odin does. I do not share this enthusiasm, as you may imagine. So far as I can remember, I have never found anyone in all the nine worlds to admire; and I hate their meek Baldr as much as they love him. Some time ago their favourite had bad dreams, and had them so repeatedly that Father Odin and Mother Frigg, becoming alarmed for their darling, called a council of the gods, consulted wise giants, and finally made all living creatures, and even the plants and metals, swear not to harm Baldr.

'Not satisfied with this, Odin visited the lower world and consulted a Vala, long since dead, concerning his son's fate. I overheard him telling Frigg about his journey. He rode on Sleipnir. When he was near the cave that leads to the world of torture, a dog met him, and barked furiously – a bad sign, I believe. I lost what came next. But at last he reached the grave of the Vala, who, I assure you, was not pleased to be disturbed after her long sleep under the dew and the snow. She told Odin that a place was being made ready for his son in the lower world. I did not hear all, but I am convinced that Odin got little comfort from his journey.

'This meek Baldr now parades his superiority by standing up as a mark for the Æsir. He thinks himself safe now; but I happen to possess a little secret of great importance. Mother Frigg, in her innocence, confided it to me, taking me for a beggar-woman. When she made all creatures swear not to harm Baldr, there was one she neglected because it was so weak, so powerless to harm anyone.

It was the little shrub mistletoe that grew on the eastern side of Valhalla. Of course, I at once secured the plant, and here it is.' And Loki drew from his bosom the withered mistletoe.

'Now for my plot, friend Thiassi! From this weak plant, you, with your wonderful skill, can make an arrow that will kill the fair-faced Baldr, the darling of the gods.' Thiassi pondered a moment, and then said, 'I would not do so much to please you. You are in my power, and I can compel you to help me whether you will or not. But I like your plot. Give me the mistletoe. The arrow I make shall be deadly; for it shall be poisoned by hate. I have already made a fatal sword whose edge the Æsir shall feel some day. Mimir the wise took it from me while I slept. I know not where it is; but it will surely fulfil the end for which it was made.'

Before they parted, it was arranged that Loki should entice Idunn outside the walls of Asgard, so that Thiassi could carry her off to Jötunheim. And Thiassi, as he flew towards the north, bore with him the withered mistletoe from which he was to make the fatal arrow.

THIASSI CARRIES OFF IDUNN

as told by Mary Litchfield

Idunn was sitting in her garden one afternoon, when Loki wandered in, and threw himself down on a low seat. All the gods came often to see Idunn. It was a charming spot, this garden, with its fountains and bowers, and Idunn was a lovely goddess. But the gods had another reason for coming – they came to get Idunn's apples.

These apples were the most delicious fruit. They were golden in colour, just touched with red; and one seemed to be eating whatever one liked best in the world when one tasted them. And there was something still more wonderful about them. Whoever ate them, if old, grew young, and if tired, felt as fresh as though just awaking from sleep. Because of these virtues, the Æsir prized them above all their treasures.

As Loki sat there, Thor, the strong god of thunder, came for refreshment after fighting with the giants in Jötunheim. Baldr the Beautiful came; for even he needed to taste the wondrous fruit. In a moment Tyr walked up, strong and cheerful in spite of the loss of his right hand.

Later came Frigg and some of the other goddesses. And all talked pleasantly together as they strolled about among the trees, or rested in the shady bowers.

Loki chuckled as he thought to himself, 'How will mighty Thor feel when his hand is too weak to fling the hammer at the giants? And how will Frigg look, when she can no longer stand erect, queen of the gods, but must totter about, a bent old woman? Oh, it will be rare sport!'

The gods came and went, and the shadows lengthened, but still Loki lingered. When at last he was alone with Idunn, he said carelessly, 'Let me see one of your apples a moment; I wish to examine it.' After looking at it critically, he smelt it and tasted it. Then he said, in a decided tone, 'Yes, it is as I thought; those apples are much finer!'

Idunn looked at him with an expression of bewilderment.

He continued: 'The gold is brighter, and the red a more beautiful shade; and the flavour is beyond that of anything I have ever tasted. I would never have believed there were apples better than yours in all the nine worlds, had I not seen and tasted them myself.'

As Loki talked, amazement and anxiety were pictured on Idunn's face; and when he finished, she burst out, 'Why, Loki! What do you mean? There cannot be apples better than mine! All the gods say so – even Odin himself; and he has been everywhere.'

'So the gods say, but how can they prove it?' said Loki, smiling. 'I have seen finer ones and have eaten them. They grow just beyond the wall and river of Asgard, in a grove. No one would ever think of looking there for apples. I found them by chance, the other day, when searching for something I had lost.'

'O Loki!' cried Idunn, with tears in her eyes. 'I cannot bear to think there are apples better than mine. I wonder if they are also apples of youth?'

'As to that I cannot say,' replied the god; 'I only know that I was quite exhausted when I came upon them, and the first taste made me feel as fresh as a lark. So I presume they surpass your apples in their youth-giving and refreshing qualities as well as in other things. However,' he added, seeing Idunn's look of distress, 'you need not be alarmed. I know how sad a thing it would be for you to lose your position as sole possessor of the wonderful fruit. And so, out of consideration for you, I have spoken to no one of my discovery. You, charming Idunn, who have always been so gracious and so generous in dispensing your treasure, you alone must have the new golden apples!'

'How kind you are, Loki!' said Idunn, the tears still in her eyes. 'Won't you get me some of them, so that I can see for myself how much better they are? I feel as though I cannot wait!'

'Let me think,' said Loki, meditatively; 'I must start for Midgard tonight. How can I manage it?' Then in a moment, he added: 'I should not have time to get the apples and come back here with them; but this is what we can do. You go with me. I shall have time to see you safely into Asgard again; and once inside the walls, you will not mind coming home alone. Or, if you prefer, you need not go outside at all. I will get the apples while you wait inside. You can decide which you would rather do when we get there.'

The unsuspecting Idunn prepared to go with Loki. She threw over her shoulders a light green mantle, her flower-embroidered robe showing gaily below it. Then she said, 'I wonder whether I had better hide my apples, or take them with me.'

'Oh, take them,' Loki replied, 'and then you won't be worrying about them.'

They started off, Idunn half frightened and half pleased at the prospect of so long a trip; for she rarely left her own home, and had not been beyond the walls for years.

'I wonder what Bragi will say if he comes back and does not find me,' she murmured. 'I hope I shall get home before dark!' And she was almost ready to turn back. But Loki was very gay, and his jests and stories soon made her forget her fears.

After a long walk – and gods walk much faster than mortals – they reached the walls of the city.

'Now,' said Loki, 'which will you do? Stay here or go with me? It makes no difference, unless you would like to see the apples growing; and possibly you may not fancy being left by yourself in such a lonely spot.'

'I am a little afraid to stay here alone,' said Idunn, 'and I should like to see the apples growing. I think I will go with you. There can't be any harm in my going if it is so near.'

Loki helped her over the high wall. And, strange to say, there was a curious boat just where they got down on the other side. Had Idunn been in the least suspicious, she might have wondered at its being there. She did not stop to wonder, but stepped in with Loki. The boat went over the rushing river with its dangerous mists as easily as a swan crosses a smooth lake. For, in truth, it was no common boat, but one made by Thiassi for this very occasion.

As they stepped on shore, Loki pointed to a grove of trees, saying, 'The apples are in there.'

They went toward the grove, and soon the long rays of the afternoon sun were shut out by the trees and the thick undergrowth.

Idunn was tired, and said in a weary tone, 'Is it much further, Loki?'

'No, only a little way,' he replied; 'but if you are tired, here is a nice mossy seat in this little opening. You can rest a few moments, while I go and get some water from the spring that bubbles out from the other side of the large rock yonder.'

Idunn sat down, holding her basket of golden apples in her lap, and leaning her beautiful head against a tree. Looking up through the opening, she could see the white clouds sailing lazily in the deep blue sky. In a few moments her eyes closed, and she was fast asleep.

She was suddenly awakened by a whirring sound, and when she looked up, the blue sky had vanished, and a dark thunder cloud was coming rapidly towards the opening.

'Loki! Loki! Come back!' she cried.

There was no reply, and the cloud came swiftly down. As it touched the tree-tops, a few feathers fell into Idunn's lap; and as she gazed in fear and wonder, it took the form of a large eagle with shining eyes. Idunn screamed with terror, and sank back helpless upon the mossy seat. As the eagle seized her, a small arrow dropped upon the ground near where she had been sitting.

Idunn was borne rapidly away toward Jötunheim. When the eagle was so far up that he looked no larger than a swallow, a form appeared from behind the large rock, and Loki, a look of malicious triumph in his face, picked up the mistletoe arrow.

THE GODS GROW OLD

as told by Mary Litchfield

When Bragi,[8] Idunn's husband, came home that night, his wife was not at the gate to meet him with her happy face and her golden hair. He searched for her in the garden and in the palace; he enquired of the people about the place, of her maidens and finally of all the gods and goddesses; but no one had seen Idunn since they left her, as well and as happy as ever, in the afternoon. Thor did remember that when he left the garden, Loki sat on a low seat, half asleep.

'Thor,' said Bragi, 'if there is mischief, Loki is at the bottom of it! Let us find him!'

They went to Loki's home, and found him sitting by a large fire. He seemed surprised to see them, and opened his eyes wide when they told him that Idunn had disappeared.

'That is very strange!' said he. 'I was the last one to leave the garden, and everything was all right then. I have seen nothing that looked suspicious near Asgard.' Then, after a short pause, he added, 'I did notice a large eagle as I walked home; but I do not think he came very near.'

---

8. The god of poetry; the best of *skalds*.

Loki seemed so innocent that they could not suspect him of knowing anything more of Idunn's whereabouts than they did.

That night and the day following, and every day, the search for Idunn was kept up; but no trace of her could be found. Great sorrow was felt throughout the city of the gods. With her, the warm summer, which never left that happy home, departed, giving place to dreary November. Cold winds blew from the north, chilling the delicate flowers. A look of decay came over the hills and fields; and yellow leaves fell from the trees, leaving them bare and brown. Vines that had always borne fruit and flowers during every month of the year rattled their lifeless stems against the tottering walls. A cold breath touched the ponds and streams, covering them with a thin coating of ice. And the birds left for the first time the summer-land of the gods and flew toward the south. The sun itself shone with a pale, sickly light, scarcely warming the blood even at noon. And the nights grew long and dark.

But if nature mourned for Idunn, the gods felt her loss still more. As long as she gave them her golden apples, weariness and old age could not touch them. Each one enjoyed the fullest life. After Idunn's going, Odin, the wise All-Father, grew older: his beard became as white as the beard of Mimir, and there was a look of sadness on his kingly features. Stately Frigg, the mother of the gods, became wrinkled and grey. Even Thor, the mighty thunder-god, showed signs of age, although his spirit was unbroken. Matters were fast becoming so desperate that Odin decided to call a council to consider what could be done to remedy the evil.

The gods and goddesses assembled – those whose homes were far away as well as those who lived in Asgard. All came except Heimdall, who could not leave his post as guardian of the bridge Bifröst. Njörd came from his wind-blown palace by the sea, 'on a strand outside of which the swans sing', in the western part of the lower world. Freyr came from Alfheim, the land of the light elves; and Vidar the Silent left his lonely vine-grown home, deep in the mountains, at the call of Odin. All came, and all showed the signs of weakness and of age.

One alone was absent when the Æsir were assembled. Loki was not there. And it had been remarked that he seemed little affected by Idunn's absence. His hair gleamed red and fiery, unmixed with grey; and his restless eyes had lost none of their brightness.

All were silent until Odin arose, feeble yet majestic, his countenance lit by the wisdom for which he had paid so dear. 'My children,' he said, 'Idunn has gone, and the world is growing old. The gods grow feeble. Winter winds already howl around Gladsheim. The shadow of death is upon us. Who will bring back Idunn?'

As he finished speaking, a god rose from his seat. He was one that was not often among them; for he lived far from Gladsheim, near the high wall of Asgard.

'May I speak, father Odin?' he asked.

Odin bowed his head; and he went on: 'I heard in my lonely home that Idunn had gone; but it did not occur to me until recently that certain strange things I had seen could have anything to do with her disappearance. What I have to say may unravel the mystery.

'One afternoon, rather late, I climbed the high wall which is near my castle, and looked down upon the dark Asgard river. Suddenly my attention was attracted by a peculiar whirring sound, such as is made by a bird in rapid flight. Looking up, I saw an enormous eagle carrying something in his talons. I could not tell what. I watched him until he became a mere speck and at last vanished on the northern horizon. On looking down, I saw another strange sight – a singular boat that crossed the dangerous river as easily as though it had been a common stream. Night was coming on, but I could distinguish Loki as he leaped from the boat, concealed it amid some bushes, and then quickly climbed the wall and went towards the centre of Asgard. I do not see Loki here, and that makes it seem still more probable that he had something to do with Idunn's disappearance.'

As the god sat down, Thor sprang up, the old fire flashing in his eyes. 'Odin,' he cried, 'shall not Bragi and I seek Loki? He shall pay dearly for it, if he is the cause of all this!'

Odin gave his permission, and they left the hall. They soon came back bringing Loki, who put on an air of careless gaiety, ill-suited to the occasion. Odin calmly repeated what the god had said, and Loki, finding it useless to deny that he had crossed the river with Idunn, told the whole story: how he was captured by Thiassi on the day when he suddenly disappeared while travelling with Odin and the other god, and how to save himself he had betrayed Idunn into Thiassi's hands.

Thor advanced towards the guilty god with his hammer raised; and then Loki, thoroughly frightened, begged for mercy, saying he would surely find a way to bring back Idunn, if they would only give him time.

'Loki,' said Odin, sternly, 'we will give you time; but if at the end of one month you do not bring her back, you shall be put to death with terrible tortures.'

Loki asked for a moment's silence, that he might think of some way in which he could outwit Thiassi. This was not an easy thing to do, because the latter was a great magician. He buried his face in his hands, but in an instant looked up, saying: 'I have a plan, but a disguise is needful. If Freyja will lend me her falcon plumage, I will match Thiassi with his eagle feathers.' And he laughed gleefully at the thought of outwitting the great artist. Then he continued: 'I know some runes by which I can change Idunn into a nut, so that I can easily bring her back. Let me go; I long to fool the giant who trailed me over the rocks and trees.'

The gods looked coldly on Loki; for they saw that his chief desire was not to rescue Idunn.

A little later a falcon might have been seen flying towards the desolate mountains of Jötunheim.

LOKI BRINGS BACK IDUNN

as told by Mary Litchfield

The home where Thiassi now lived was in Jötunheim, a land inhabited by giants. This region was separated from Midgard by the great river, Ocean, and lay between Asgard and the lower world. After the gods pronounced in favour of the dwarfs, Thiassi came here and shut himself up in a grim stone castle, where he spent most of his time making weapons to be used against his foes. His dwelling was near the sea, and rose like a jagged mountain amid the grey rocks of the coast. A few stunted trees and bushes clung to crevices in the rocks, and in the valleys were scanty patches of coarse grass. A dull twilight reigned always, and over all hung a leaden sky.

Loki's flight was very rapid, and it did not take him long to reach Jötunheim, although it was so far from Asgard. As he neared the coast, he made large circles, flying far out to sea. There he saw Thiassi fishing – a most fortunate thing; for had he been at home, it would have been hard for Loki to reach Idunn without his knowledge.

Next he circled around the castle, coming nearer each time, and examining it carefully on every side. As he passed by one of the rude openings that served as windows, a gleam like sunshine shot out into the grey twilight. Loki alighted on the edge and looked in. There, on a rough couch, lay Idunn, sleeping. There were tears on her cheeks, and the basket of golden apples was clasped firmly to her breast. Her long yellow hair filled the bare room with radiance, and the light streamed out through the opening, making a little sunshine in that land of gloom. In her sleep she sobbed, and Loki caught the word 'Asgard'.

Losing no time, he flew into the room, and taking his proper shape, gently awakened her. She stared vacantly for a moment, and then fear and reproach pictured themselves upon her face. 'False Loki!' she cried. 'Why are you here? Through you I am a prisoner far from Asgard!'

'Do not waste time in reproaches, fair Idunn,' said Loki. 'I alone can save you; and I will, if you do as I bid you.' Seeing the look of distrust still on Idunn's face, he added: 'You may trust me; for if I do not carry you safely back to Asgard, I am to be put to death with dreadful tortures. All the gods are growing old, and Asgard is desolate. You may thank me, after all; they will think more of you than ever when you go back with your precious fruit.'

So Idunn's fears were quieted; and as there was no other hope of escape, she decided to trust herself to Loki.

'Now,' said he, 'grasp your basket firmly, while I say some runes that will make you as small as a nut. In that way, I can carry you safely home.' Idunn did as Loki bade her, although she trembled as she felt herself growing smaller and smaller. Loki again put on his falcon plumage, and in an instant was flying towards the south. He felt quite sure that Thiassi had not seen him.

He flew more swiftly than the hawk that seeks his prey, or than the eagle that returns to her young. From time to time he turned his head to see if Thiassi, in his eagle plumage, were following him. He had gone so far that the huge castle could hardly be seen on the horizon, when above it appeared a small black speck. It was Thiassi.

The race now began in earnest. Both flew steadily for hours, high up among the leaden clouds of the cheerless sky. Loki put forth his godlike strength, and Thiassi his giant force. At last the glittering towers of Asgard gleamed against the southern sky. Would Loki reach it in time?

In the city of the gods all was expectancy from the time Loki set forth. Wily and skilful they knew him to be, but Thiassi was fierce and powerful. The result was doubtful. The gods gathered near the wall of Asgard that looked toward Jötunheim. Odin, only, sat apart, far up in his High Seat. In the dim distance he could see the mountains and castles of Jötunheim. Cold winds blew, and Asgard looked cheerless in the waning light of the afternoon. Beautiful as ever rose the stately homes of the gods; but the plains of Ida lay brown and bare, except for a few scattered snowflakes. No summer sounds were in the air; for all the birds had flown, and even the song of the cricket was hushed.

Odin kept his eyes fixed upon the distant mountains, that he might catch the first glimpse of the returning Loki. He knew, better than anyone else, the vast importance of Loki's errand; and his face, grown old and lined with care, expressed the great anxiety he felt. His ravens had not come back from their daily journey, but the two wolves lay at his feet, watching his countenance with eager eyes: near him stood Hermod, the messenger god.

Suddenly a gleam shot across the stern face of the All-Father, and a light like the fire of battle shone in his eyes. 'Go, Hermod!' he cried. 'Tell the Æsir, Loki comes! But stay,' he added; and then in a moment, 'say Thiassi, clad in his eagle plumage, pursues him! The gods will soon see them from the wall of Asgard.'

Hermod hastened to tell the gods, and more eagerly than ever did they scan the northern horizon for the wished-for sight.

Hermod went back to Odin, but soon rejoined the gods, saying: 'The All-Father gave Loki important instructions before he left Asgard. He bade him lower his flight as he neared the city, for the mists of the rushing river cannot harm him; but should Thiassi fly low enough, they will burst into flames, since he is now an enemy to the Æsir.'

In a moment two specks could be seen in the north. Then what suspense was felt by the gods! Every eye was fixed upon the swiftly advancing birds. The Æsir showed signs of weakness, as they stood there, and looked older by years than when Idunn left them. The chill wind whistled through their garments; but they did not feel it. Nor did they see the sun as he sank wearily behind the dark clouds in the west, as though he too had grown old. One thought alone filled all their minds – could Loki hold out? Would he reach Asgard before the powerful Thiassi, who seemed to be gaining upon him?

Nearer and nearer comes Loki. His flight is very swift; and although the eagle is gaining upon him, the distance is short. Will he remember to lower his flight? Yes; he suddenly swoops down as he nears the dark river. The gods stand breathless, with outstretched arms. Thiassi, too, lowers his flight, forgetting the dangerous mists. At last Loki is over the river and over the wall, and now he falls exhausted to the ground. But the gods heed him not, so intently are they watching Thiassi. As the eagle flies over the river, the mists burst into fierce flames, burning his wings; but he can neither stop nor turn back, his headway is so great. His scorched wings bear him over the wall, and he falls dead in their midst.

As the gods turn to look at Loki, they behold him in his natural form, and near him stands Idunn, radiant with joy, holding out with her old gracious smile her basket of golden apples. The sun, as though suddenly grown young, sends a parting stream of radiance from the west; the clouds are turned to gold; Gladsheim glitters in the distance. Youth and summer have come back to the home of the gods.

SKADI'S CHOICE

as told by Abbie Farewell Brown

The giant Thiassi, whom Thor slew for the theft of Idunn and the magic apples, had a daughter, Skadi, who was a very good sort of girl, as giantesses go. Most of them were evil-tempered, spiteful and cruel creatures, who desired only to do harm to the gods and to all who were good. But Skadi was different. Stronger than the hatred of her race for the Æsir, stronger even than her wish to be revenged for her father's death, was her love for Baldr the Beautiful, the pride of all the gods. If she had not been a giantess, she might have hoped that he would love her also; but she knew that no one who lived in Asgard would ever think kindly of her race, which had caused so much trouble to Baldr and his brothers. After her father was killed by the Æsir, however, Skadi had a wise idea.

Skadi put on her helm and corselet and set out for Asgard, meaning to ask a noble price to pay for the sorrow of Thiassi's death. The gods, who had all grown young and boyish once again, were sitting in Valhalla merrily enjoying a banquet in honour of Idunn's safe return when Skadi, clattering with steel, strode into their midst. Heimdal the watchman, astonished at the sight, had let this maiden warrior pass him upon the rainbow bridge. The Æsir set down their cups hastily, and the laughter died upon their lips; for though she looked handsome, Skadi was a terrible figure in her silver armour and with her spear as long as a ship's mast brandished in her giant hand.

The nine Valkyries, Odin's maiden warriors, hurried away to put on their own helmets and shields; for they would not have this other maiden, ten times as huge, see them meekly waiting at table, while they had battle-dresses as fine as hers to show the stranger.

'Who are you, maiden, and what seek you here?' asked Father Odin.

'I am Skadi, the daughter of Thiassi, whom your folk have slain,' answered she, 'and I come here for redress.'

At these words the coward Loki, who had been at the killing of Thiassi, skulked low behind the table; but Thor, who had done the killing, straightened himself and clenched his fists tightly. He was not afraid of any giant, however fierce, and this maiden with her shield and spear only angered him.

'Well, Skadi,' quoth Odin gravely, 'your father was a thief, and died for his sins. He stole fair Idunn and her magic apples, and for that crime he died, which was only just. Yet because our righteous deed has left you an orphan, Skadi, we will grant you a recompense, so you shall be at peace with us; for it is not fitting that the Æsir should quarrel with women. What is it you ask, O Skadi, as solace for the death of Thiassi?'

Skadi looked like an orphan who was well able to take care of herself; and this indeed her next words showed her to be. 'I ask two things,' she said, without a moment's hesitation: 'I ask the husband whom I shall select from among you; and I ask that you shall make me laugh, for it is many days since grief has let me enjoy a smile.'

At this strange request the Æsir looked astonished, and some of them seemed rather startled; for you can fancy that none of them wanted a giantess, however handsome, for his wife. They put their heads together and consulted long whether or not they should allow Skadi her two wishes.

'I will agree to make her laugh,' grinned Loki; 'but suppose she should choose me for her husband! I am married to one giantess already.'

'No fear of that, Loki,' said Thor; 'you were too near being the cause of her father's death for her to love you overmuch. Nor do I think that she will choose me; so I am safe.'

Loki chuckled and stole away to think up a means of making Skadi laugh.

Finally, the gods agreed that Skadi should choose one of them for her husband; but in order that all might have a fair chance of missing this honour which no one coveted, she was to choose in a curious way. All the Æsir were to stand in a row behind the curtain which was drawn across the end of the hall, so that only their feet were seen by Skadi; and by their feet alone Skadi was to select him who was to be her husband.

Now Skadi was very ready to agree to this, for she said to herself, 'Surely, I shall know the feet of Baldr, for they will be the most beautiful of any.'

Amid nervous laughter at this new game, the Æsir ranged themselves in a row behind the purple curtain, with only their line of feet showing below the golden border. There were Father Odin, Thor the thunderer and Baldr his brother; there was old Njörd the rich, with his fair son Freyr; there were Tyr the bold, Bragi the poet, blind Höd and Vidar the silent; Vali and Ull the archers, Forseti the wise judge and Heimdal the gold-toothed watchman. Loki alone, of all the Æsir, was not there; and Loki was the only one who did not shiver as Skadi walked up and down the hall looking at the row of feet.

Up and down, back and forth, went Skadi, looking carefully;

and among all those sandalled feet there was one pair more white and fair and beautiful than the rest.

'Surely, these are Baldr's feet!' she thought, while her heart thumped with eagerness under her silver corselet. 'Oh, if I guess aright, dear Baldr will be my husband!'

She paused confidently before the handsomest pair of feet, and, pointing to them with her spear, she cried, 'I choose here! Few blemishes are to be found in Baldr the Beautiful.'

A shout of laughter arose behind the curtain, and forth slunk – not young Baldr, but old Njörd the rich, king of the ocean wind, the father of those fair twins, Freyr and Freyja. Skadi had chosen the handsome feet of old Njörd, and thenceforth he must be her husband.

Njörd was little pleased; but Skadi was heartbroken. Her face grew longer and sadder than before when he stepped up and took her hand sulkily, saying, 'Well, I am to be your husband, then, and all my riches stored in Noatûn, the home of ships, are to be yours. You would have chosen Baldr, and I wish that this luck had been his! However, it cannot be helped now.'

'Nay,' answered Skadi, frowning, 'the bargain is not yet complete. No one of you has made me laugh. I am so sad now, that it will be a merry jest indeed which can wring laughter from my heavy heart.' She sighed, looking at Baldr. But Baldr loved only Nanna in all the world.

Just then, out came Loki, riding on one of Thor's goat steeds; and the red-bearded fellow cut up such ridiculous capers with the grey-bearded goat that soon not only Skadi, but all the Æsir and Njörd himself were holding their sides with laughter.

'Fairly won, fairly won!' cried Skadi, wiping the tears from her eyes. 'I am beaten. I shall not forget that it is Loki to whom

I owe this last joke. Some day I shall be quits with you, red joker!' And this threat she carried out in the end, on the day of Loki's punishment.

Skadi was married to old Njörd, both unwilling; and they went to live among the mountains in Skadi's home, which had once been Thiassi's palace, where he had shut Idunn in a prison cell. As you can imagine, Njörd and Skadi did not live happily ever after, like the good prince and princess in the story-book. For, in the first place, Skadi was a giantess; and there are few folk, I fancy, who could live happily with a giantess. In the second place, she did not love Njörd, nor did he love Skadi, and neither forgot that Skadi's choosing had been sorrow to them both. But the third reason was the most important of all; and this was because Skadi and Njörd could not agree upon the place which should be their home. For Njörd did not like the mountain palace of Skadi's people – the place where roaring winds rushed down upon the sea and its ships. The sea with its ships was his friend, and he wanted to dwell in Noatûn, where he had greater wealth than anyone else in the world – where he could rule the fresh sea-wind and tame the wild ocean, granting the prayers of fisher-folk and the seafarers, who loved his name.

Finally, they agreed to dwell first in one place, then in the other, so that each might be happy in turn. For nine days they tarried in Thrymheim, and then they spent three in Noatûn. But even this arrangement could not bring peace. One day they had a terrible quarrel. It was just after they had come down from Skadi's mountain home for their three days in Njörd's sea palace, and he was so glad to be back that he cried:

'Ah, how I hate your hills! How long the nine nights seemed, with the wolves howling until dawn among the dark mountains of

Giant Land! What a discord compared to the songs of the swans who sail upon my dear, dear ocean!' Thus rudely he taunted his wife; but Skadi answered him with spirit.

'And I – I cannot sleep by your rolling sea-waves, where the birds are ever calling, calling, as they come from the woods on the shore. Each morning the seagull's scream wakes me at some unseemly hour. I will not stay here even for three nights! I will not stay!'

'And I will have no more of your windy mountain-tops,' roared Njörd, beside himself with rage. 'Go, if you wish! Go back to Thrymheim! I shall not follow you, be sure!'

So Skadi went back to her mountains alone, and dwelt in the empty house of Thiassi, her father. She became a mighty huntress, swift on the skis and ice-runners which she strapped to her feet. Day after day she skimmed over the snow-crusted mountains, bow in hand, to hunt the wild beasts which roamed there. 'Ski-goddess' she was called; and never again did she come to Asgard halls. Quite alone in the cold country, she hunted hardily, keeping ever in her heart the image of Baldr the Beautiful, whom she loved, but whom she had lost forever by her unlucky choice.

GEIRRÖD AND AGNAR

as told by by Sarah Powers Bradish

I. THE LITTLE PRINCES

Odin and Frigg from their lofty seat often looked down into the palace of a certain king. They came to be very fond of the two little sons of this king.

One day the little princes went out in a boat to fish. A storm came up suddenly. Their boat drifted out to sea. It was thrown by the waves on an island, where an old couple lived in a cottage. The old people, who were Odin and Frigg in disguise, took the princes home and cared for them.

They were very kind to both children; but the elder, Geirröd, was Odin's favourite; while the younger, Agnar, appealed to Frigg's motherly heart. They lived contentedly with their friends during the cold, dark winter. But when the long, bright days of spring came, and the sea grew calm, and the skies were blue, they longed for their father and mother and the playmates in their distant home. So Odin gave them a boat, and sent them away under favourable winds.

They made the voyage quickly; but, when the boat touched the shore of their native land, Geirröd leaped out; and, pushing the boat back into the water, left Agnar to the mercy of the waves.

Geirröd hastened to his father's house, where he was welcomed as one brought back from the dead. But little Agnar drifted away to the land of the giants. He fell into the hands of good giants, who gave him a home, where he lived many years. When he became a man, he married a young giantess, and settled down to stay with his benefactors. But, after a time, he longed to see his own people. So he built a boat, and sailed away over the sea.

He found his native land; but the king, his father, was dead; and his brother, Geirröd, was king instead. Geirröd received his brother as a subject, and made him a servant in his father's palace.

II. THE SELFISH KING

Frigg had been watching the two princes all the time. She saw how unjust and cruel Geirröd was to his younger brother. Odin knew only of Geirröd's success, and admired him as a great king.

One day, when Odin and Frigg were sitting on their lofty seat, looking out over the world, Odin said, 'See what a mighty king Geirröd has become, while your little pet, Agnar, is nothing but the little husband of a giantess.'

'True,' said Frigg, 'but Geirröd, with all his grandeur, is mean and selfish. He is even guilty of inhospitality, an offence most shameful in a Norseman. But Agnar, in his poverty, is still kind and generous.'

Odin said he would test Geirröd's hospitality. He put on his cloud cloak and broad-brimmed hat, and set out to visit Geirröd. In the meantime, Frigg sent word to Geirröd that he must be watchful, because a wicked enchanter was approaching his palace.

When Odin arrived, he gave his name as Grimnir, and refused to tell who he was or whence he came. Thinking that the old man must be the wicked enchanter, Geirröd ordered his servants to bind him and place him between two fires that were burning on the floor of his great hall. The fires scorched the old man's face, but did not burn his garments. There he stayed eight days and nights, in silence and without food. He would have had nothing to drink, but for Agnar, who secretly brought him a drinking horn containing a refreshing draught.

III. AGNAR'S REWARD

At the close of the eighth day, Geirröd was seated on his throne, enjoying the sight of his guest's sufferings, when the old man began to sing. The song was faint at first, but grew louder and louder, until the chains dropped away, the fires went out, and the feeble old man stood up in the beauty and strength of a god. In his song, Odin told how the king, who had been so blessed by the gods, should fall by his own sword.

Geirröd was about to slay the unwelcome guest; but, as he rose from his seat, his foot slipped, and he fell on his sword, as had just been foretold.

Odin placed Agnar on the throne, and blessed him with great wealth and happiness.

FREYR

as told by Sarah Powers Bradish

I. FREYR'S GIFTS

Njord had two children: a boy named Freyr, and a girl named Freyja. Freyr was the god of sunlight and gentle showers, and Freyja was the goddess of beauty.

It was the custom in the Northland to make every child a present when he cut his first tooth. When Freyr's first tooth came through, the gods gave him Elfheim, the home of the light elves, or fairies, for a tooth gift. The little god was king of Elfheim, or Fairyland, and lived there with his tiny subjects, whenever he could be spared from Asgard. The little creatures loved their king, and obeyed his lightest wish; and he was much happier there than in his mother's icy palace at Thrymheim.

Little Freyr soon became a tall, handsome youth. Then the gods gave him a magic sword, which, as soon as it was drawn from the sheath, won every battle of its own accord. But Freyr seldom used it, except to fight the cruel frost giants, who dreaded his glittering sword, because it held the softening power of the sunbeams.

Freyr had also a fine horse called Blodughofi. This horse could go through fire and water.

II. FREYR IN ODIN'S SEAT

Freyr was very busy during the summer months. He looked after the sunshine and the warm showers. Sometimes he helped his father direct the gentle winds. But, when the sunshine went away, Freyr's work went away too. The dark northern winter seemed very long to the young god.

One day, when wandering about the city of Asgard, he came to the foot of Odin's lofty throne, Hlidskialf. No one ever ascended this throne, except the All-Father and his wife Frigg. But the gods all knew that the whole world could be seen from its summit. Freyr wanted to see the whole world. So he began to climb the steps. No one saw him, and he soon came to the top. He sat down on Odin's seat, and looked toward the north. He saw a maiden standing in the doorway of her father's castle. She was the most beautiful maiden in the world. She was Gerda, daughter of Gymir, the frost giant. When she raised her hand to open the door, many-coloured lights blazed in the northern sky, and shot out toward the southern heavens. Freyr longed to win Gerda for his bride.

But he knew that her father, Gymir, would never consent to their marriage, because Gymir was cousin to Thiassi, the storm giant, whom the gods had killed in Asgard. Slowly and sadly Freyr left Hlidskialf. He walked up and down the city streets as usual; but he was silent, and never joined in the sports of the young gods. At the feasts his cup of sparkling mead was left untasted. No one could find out any reason for his strange conduct. His father, Njörd, was greatly alarmed, and sent for his stepmother Skadi, who was then at their winter home in Thrymheim.

III. HOW SKADI HELPED HER STEPSON

Skadi came at once. She, too, was greatly concerned about her stepson. She knew there must be some trouble; but he refused to tell his stepmother what it was that made him so miserable.

One day Skadi called Skirnir, their most trusted servant. She said: 'Skirnir, you played with Freyr in childhood; you were his friend in youth; you have served him faithfully in manhood. He trusts you. Find out his secret, and help him in his trouble. You alone can save his life.'

Skirnir went to Freyr, and learned from him the story of his visit to the lofty throne, how he had seen Gerda, the most beautiful of maidens, and how he wished to make her his wife. This, Freyr said, could never be done, because Gerda was the daughter of Gymir, the frost giant, who hated him. Besides, the giant's castle was surrounded by a barrier of fire, and at the approach of any stranger the flames leaped as high as the sky.

'If that is all,' said Skirnir, 'I can win fair Gerda for you. Lend me your horse, Blodughofi, and give me your magic sword to be my own.'

Freyr lent him the horse and gave him the sword; and Skirnir promised to hasten on his journey.

Freyr sent eleven golden apples and a magic golden ring, as gifts to Gerda. Still Skirnir lingered.

One day, as Freyr was sitting near a pool, his face was reflected in the surface. Skirnir caught the reflection in his drinking horn, and covered it carefully. Then he started on his journey; for, with these three gifts, the golden apples, the magic ring and the portrait of his handsome master, he was confident that he could win the beautiful maiden.

IV. SKIRNIR'S JOURNEY

Skirnir rode away to the land of the frost giants as fast as Freyr's swift steed could carry him. As he came near Gymir's castle, he was stopped by the terrible howling of the giant's watchdogs, Winter Winds.

He spoke to the shepherd who was watching the flocks in Gymir's fields. The shepherd said: 'You cannot reach the castle. Even if you pass the dogs, it will be impossible for you to enter the gates, for the whole place is surrounded by fire. Don't you see how the flames light up the sky?'

Still Skirnir pressed on. He put spurs to his horse, and outran the dogs. Then he gave rein to Blodughofi, who plunged into the fire and bore his rider safely to the steps of Gymir's castle. A servant opened the door and led the daring horseman into the presence of Gerda.

Skirnir offered her the golden apples and the magic ring, and showed her the portrait of his master, which he had taken from the pool. But she said, 'My father has gold enough for me,' and she did not care at all for the picture.

Then Skirnir threatened to cut off her head with the magic sword. He did not intend to do this, because he knew his master would not want a bride without a head. But she was not at all frightened. Then he cut runes in his stick, so that he could weave a magic spell about her. He told her that she would be married to an old frost giant, who would keep her hidden in his cold, dark castle. He kept on cutting runes until she said: 'Perhaps it would be better to marry handsome young Freyr and live in Asgard, than to marry an ugly old frost giant and live in a dungeon. When spring comes, I will be Freyr's bride.'

Skirnir hurried back toward Asgard. But Freyr, impatient to learn how he had succeeded, met him at Elfheim, and there, among the fairies, he learned that, when the trees budded and flowers bloomed and grass grew green again, he might go to the land of Buri, or green groves, to meet his bride.

Gerda met him in the land of Buri, as she had promised. They were married, and went to Freyr's new palace in Asgard, where they lived happily ever after, and blessed the homes of married pairs who wished to live without strife.

V. PEACE-FRODI

Freyr had a son named Frodi. Frodi lived in Midgard, or the world of men. He was good and wise, and men were glad to have him for a king. He began to reign in Denmark, when there was peace throughout the world. That was the time when Christ was born in Bethlehem. He was called Peace-Frodi.

He had a pair of magic millstones. They could grind anything he wished, but there was no one in all his kingdom strong enough to turn them. He went to visit the king of Sweden, and saw, near the royal palace, two captive giants, who were eight feet tall. They could lift heavy weights, and hurl javelins to a great distance. He thought they would be able to turn his enchanted millstones. He bought the giants from their master. Their names were Menia and Fenia.

As soon as they came to Denmark, Frodi led them to the magic stones and bade them grind gold, peace and prosperity. They turned the stones easily, and sang as they worked:

'Let us grind riches for Frodi!
Let us make him happy
In plenty of substance
On our magic Quern.'[9]

They worked on hour after hour until their backs ached, and they could hardly stand from weariness. There was peace in the world, prosperity in the land, and the king's treasuries were filled with gold. The king had always been kind and gentle, but he was maddened by the sight of the gold, and, when the women begged to be allowed to rest, he sharply bade them work on. 'Rest as long as the cuckoo is silent in the spring,' he said. 'Alas,' they replied, 'the cuckoo is never silent in the spring.' When they could work no longer, he gave them as much time to rest as would be required to sing one verse of their song.

But while Frodi slept, they changed their song, and began to grind an armed host, instead of gold.

They sang:

'An army must come
Hither forthwith,
And burn the town
For the prince.'[10]

---

9. Longfellow's translation, *Grotta Savngr*.

10. Longfellow's translation, *Grotta Savngr*.

A viking landed with his soldiers, and surprised the Danes. He defeated Frodi's army, and carried away the Danish treasure. He took Menia and Fenia, with their magic millstones, on board his own ship. He ordered them to grind salt, instead of gold. But he was as greedy as Frodi had become. He kept the giants at work until they were worn out. But they had already ground so much salt that its weight caused the ship to sink, and all on board perished. As the millstones sank, the water, rushing in, gurgled through the holes in the millstones, and made a great whirlpool. This whirlpool is off the northwestern coast of Norway, and is still known as the Maelstrom.

The salt dissolved and made all the water very salt, and the water of the sea is salt to this day.

VI. YULETIDE

Skirnir kept Freyr's magic sword for his own, and he did not bring back the borrowed horse, Blodughofi. So, for a long time, Freyr had neither sword nor horse. The dwarfs kindly supplied him with a swift steed, as we shall see. This was a boar called Gullinbursti, or Golden-bristle, which was, ever after, Freyr's constant attendant. The golden bristles gave light, and were the rays of the sun; or, some say, the golden grain, which grew in Midgard, at the sun-god's bidding. Gullinbursti, by tearing up the earth with his tusks, taught men to plough. Sometimes Freyr rode on his back; and sometimes he harnessed him to his chariot, from which he scattered fruits and flowers, as he drove over the world. Sometimes his sister Freyja rode with him in his chariot, and helped him in blessing men with fruits.

Boar's flesh was eaten at the festivals sacred to Freyr. The roasted boar's head, crowned with laurel and rosemary, was brought into the dining room with great ceremony. The head of the household laid his hand upon it, and swore that he would be faithful to his family and true to his promises. Then everyone present followed his example.

The boar's head was then carved by a man of good character and great courage.

The helmets of Northern warriors were often ornamented with boars' heads, because that emblem of the conquering sun-god was supposed to strike terror into the hearts of the enemy.

The longest night of the year was called Mother Night. It was a time of rejoicing, because the sun was then beginning his homeward journey. It was called Yuletide, or Wheeltide, because the sun was thought to be like a wheel rolling across the sky. A large wooden wheel was taken to the top of a high hill, wound well with straw, set on fire, and, when all ablaze, rolled down into the water, because the sight of the burning wheel suggested the sun's course through the heavens.

This Yule festival was kept in England for many years. As it occurred in the month of December, it was easily united with the festivities of Christmas.

At Yuletide, a huge log was brought in and burned in the great fireplace. It was a bad omen if it did not burn all night. In the morning, the charred pieces were gathered and saved to light the Yule log the following year.

FREYJA

as told by Sarah Powers Bradish

I. HOW GOLD CAME TO BE HIDDEN IN THE ROCKS

Freyja was the daughter of Njörd. She was the goddess of beauty. She had golden hair and blue eyes. She had a commanding figure, and was clad in flowing robes. She wore a corselet and helmet, and carried a shield and a spear. She rode in a chariot drawn by two large grey cats. She admired brave men, and liked nothing so well as to reward a deed of valour. She visited battle-fields, to choose, from the slain heroes, those who should be her guests at Folkvang, her palace in Asgard. The other slain warriors were taken to live with Odin in his great hall, Valhalla.

Folkvang was always filled with heroes and their wives and sweethearts. Northern women often rushed into battle, or fell upon swords, or were burned on the funeral pyre with their beloved dead, hoping that their courage and devotion would win Freyja's favour, so that they might enjoy the society of their husbands and lovers in Folkvang.

Freyja was married to Odur, god of the summer sun. They had two daughters, who were so beautiful that all lovely and precious things were called by their names. All beautiful creatures were said to belong to Freyja. Butterflies were called Freyja's hens. Freyja was always happy when she had her family together. But her husband, Odur, was too fond of travel. He always spent the winter in the Southland. This was a source of great grief to Freyja. Once he left home without saying where he intended to go. Freyja was heartbroken. She wept constantly. All nature wept with her. Hard rocks softened when her tears fell upon them! They opened their stony hearts to receive every shining drop, and hid it as pure gold. The sea treasured her tears, and threw them back upon the shore as clearest amber.

After long waiting, Freyja went in search of her husband. She wandered through every part of the earth, weeping as she went. The earth kept her tears as fine gold. This is the reason that gold is found in all parts of the world.

II. WHY NORTHERN BRIDES WEAR MYRTLE

Freyja found the missing Odur far away in the sunny Southland. He was sitting under a flowering myrtle tree, watching the fleecy clouds change colour in the rays of the setting sun. He was well and happy, and did not think how lonely his beautiful wife must be in the dark winter of the frozen North. But when she stood before him, he was glad to see her; and she was almost beside herself with joy.

Hand in hand, they returned to the Northland. Birds sang and flowers bloomed along their pathway, and spring followed their footsteps. Freyja wore a garland of myrtle leaves; and to this day Northern brides wear myrtle wreaths instead of orange blossoms.

III. BRISINGA-MEN

Freyja was fond of ornaments and jewels. One day, when passing through the land of the dark elves, she saw four dwarfs at work on a wonderful necklace. It was called Brisinga-men. It was an emblem of the fruitfulness of the earth. It was made of the most precious gems, which sparkled like stars. She begged the dwarfs to give her the beautiful necklace.

They said it should be hers if she would promise to grant them her favour forever. This was a great deal to ask; but the necklace was a masterpiece of art, and priceless in value. So she promised all they asked, and they clasped the necklace about her neck. She wore it night and day. Once she lent it to Thor, when he went to the land of the giants; and once she lost it; but she always regarded it as her choicest treasure.

IV. HEIMDAL SAVES BRISINGA-MEN

The gods had just finished the rainbow bridge, which they built to connect Asgard with Midgard and Urdar Fountain. This bridge was made of fire, air and water. These three things can still be seen in the rainbow; fire in the red, air in the blue and water in the green. All the gods except Thor passed over the bridge every day, on their way to their council chamber at Urdar Fountain. Thor was still obliged to harness his goats to his iron chariot and drive in the old way, because they all feared that his heavy tread and the heat of the lightnings, which always attended him, would destroy the beautiful bridge. They feared also that the giants would take advantage of the new bridge to force an entrance into Asgard. So they decided to appoint a guard for the rainbow bridge.

Heimdal was the son of the nine wave daughters of Ægir, ruler of the sea. His nine mothers fed him on the strength of the earth, the moisture of the sea and the heat of the sun. He grew very fast and could do many remarkable things. He could hear the grass growing in the fields, and the wool on the sheep's backs. He could see at a distance of one hundred miles, as clearly by night as by day. He needed less sleep than a bird. He was very beautiful, and had gold teeth which flashed when he smiled. He was always clothed in pure white, and carried a glittering sword.

The gods decided to take Heimdal to Asgard, and then they appointed him to be guard of the rainbow bridge. They built him a palace on the highest point of the bridge, and gave him a golden-maned horse called Gull-top, and a wonderful trumpet called Giallar-horn. The trumpet was to be used only when he saw the enemies of the gods approaching. Then he would know that the Twilight of the Gods was near at hand, and the sound of the trumpet would arouse all creatures in heaven and earth and the land of the mist.

One night Heimdal was disturbed by the sound of footsteps in the direction of Freyja's palace. He soon found that the noise was made by Loki, who had just changed himself into a fly, in order to enter Freyja's chamber window. Once within her room, he resumed his usual form, and tried to take the precious necklace, Brisinga-men, from her neck, as she lay asleep. Her head was turned so that he could not reach the clasp without waking her. He stepped back and muttered magic runes. He began to shrink, and shrank and shrank until he shrank into the size and shape of a flea. Then he made his way under the cover and bit Freyja's side until she turned in her sleep. He became Loki again, unclasped the necklace, and stole away.

Heimdal mounted Gull-top and galloped over the rainbow bridge. He met the robber just outside the gates of Asgard, and drew his sword. Quick as thought, Loki became a faint blue flame. Heimdal changed himself into a cloud, and poured torrents of rain upon the flame. Then the flame became a great white bear, which drank up the water. The cloud became a bear also, and the two bears fought until Loki slipped into the water in the form of a seal. Heimdal became a seal, and pursued Loki until he gave up the necklace, which was sent back to Freyja so quickly that she never knew it had been stolen.

But Heimdal had been badly hurt in his struggle with Loki. Idunn came and bound up his wounds, and healed them with a golden apple.

LOKI AND SKYRMSLI

as told by Sarah Powers Bradish

I. THE PEASANT'S TROUBLE

Loki was not always bad. He was fond of mischief, and his pranks soon grew into practical jokes. But he was kind sometimes, and generous when it did not cost too much.

Once a peasant played chess with a giant. The stake was the peasant's only son. The giant, whose name was Skyrmsli, won the game, and said he would come for the boy the next day. But if the parents could hide the child so that he could not find him, he would give up his claim.

In their distress the peasants prayed to Odin for help. The All-Father came to earth, changed the boy into a kernel of wheat, hid him in an ear of grain in a large field, and assured the anxious father and mother that the giant would not be able to find him.

The following day the giant came, searched the house, but failed to find the boy. Then he took the scythe and mowed the field of wheat. He selected a handful of ears, and chose the ear that held the enchanted kernel.

He was picking out the right grain of wheat when Odin, hearing the cry of the child, snatched him from the giant's hand and returned him to his parents. But, he said, they must take care of him now, for he could do no more.

Then they called on Odin's brother, Hoenir, who changed the boy into down, and hid him in the breast of a swan that was swimming in a pond nearby.

When the giant came, he went to the pond, caught the swan, bit off its head, and was about to swallow the down, when Hoenir wafted it away from his lips and sent it into the cottage. He gave the boy back to his parents, but declared that he could do no more.

II. LOKI COMES TO THE RESCUE

In despair, they invoked the aid of Loki, who came at once, carried the boy out to sea, changed him into a tiny egg, and hid him in the roe of a flounder. Then he rowed back to shore, where he found the giant preparing for a fishing excursion.

'Come with me,' said Loki. 'I will show you a good place to fish for herring.'

But Skyrmsli wanted to fish for flounders, and thought he could do very well alone. Loki, therefore, insisted on going with him. Skyrmsli rowed as far as he wished to go, baited his hook, caught several fish, and, at last, drew up the flounder in which Loki had concealed the precious egg. Then he rowed back to shore. Loki snatched the egg and set the boy on the landing, saying, 'Run home now; but go through the boat house and shut the door behind you.'

The frightened boy obeyed, and the giant rushed after him. But Loki had fixed a spike in the boat house so that it should strike Skyrmsli's head as he passed through. He fell; and Loki, following, cut off one of his legs.

To Loki's surprise, the pieces grew together again. He saw that it was the work of magic, but he cut off the other one, and threw a flint and steel between the leg and the body, which broke the charm, and the giant died.

The thankful parents ever after regarded Loki as the greatest of the three gods, because he had delivered them from their trouble, while the others had only helped them for a little time.

LOKI MAKES TROUBLE BETWEEN THE ARTISTS AND THE GODS

as told by Mary Litchfield

Loki once cut off the beautiful hair of Sif, Thor's wife. And when Thor found out that Loki was the culprit, he threatened to crush every bone in his body if he did not repair the mischief he had done. Loki promised to do this, for he feared Thor. He went at once to the sons of Ivaldi for help. They were famous artists, these sons of Ivaldi[11]. Many were the weapons and ornaments they had made for the gods. They quickly spun some golden hair for Sif. This wonderful hair grew to her head, becoming like her own hair, except that it was gold.

Besides this they sent a spear to Odin, and a ship to Freyr. The spear was sure to hit the mark each time; and the ship, called *Skidbladnir*, could be folded up like a napkin and put into the pocket when not in use: it would always have fair winds.

It has been told how Odin, on his journey to Mimir's well, passed near the singular hall of the dwarf Sindri and his brothers. One day when Loki was near there, it occurred to him that it would be an easy matter to stir up jealousy between the two sets of artists. Perhaps, too, he could, at the same time, make trouble between them and the gods.

---

11. The artists, the productive forces of vegetation.

One of Sindri's brothers was outside the castle as Loki came near; and the latter at once began to talk with him about the making of beautiful and curious objects. Loki described the wonderful gifts the sons of Ivaldi had sent the gods by him, and then said, 'I will wager my head that you cannot make, you and your brothers, three treasures as good as those I have just described!'

The dwarf was angry at this disparagement of their skill, and hurried into the hall to tell Sindri of Loki's wager. Loki went in after him, and repeated what he had said, adding that, if they would make the gifts, the gods themselves should be the judges, and pronounce upon the merits of the rival artists.

They went to the smithy, which was in another part of the castle. The heat from the great furnace was so intense that even Loki, who loved fire, could hardly bear it. Sindri took down a pigskin that was hanging on the wall, and putting it into the furnace, told his brother Brok to blow the bellows, and not stop blowing until he took the pigskin out.

Loki stepped behind some iron-work, and instantly a fly appeared upon the hand of Brok as he was blowing the bellows, and stung him badly; but he bore the pain, and did not stop blowing. Very soon Sindri drew from the furnace a boar with golden bristles.

Next, Sindri put some gold into the furnace, giving his brother the same directions. This time the fly settled upon Brok's neck, and stung him so that he lifted his shoulders, but still kept on blowing. The result was a ring.

The next time, Sindri put iron into the furnace; and as Brok was blowing, the fly buzzed angrily, and settling between his eyes, stung him so severely on the eyelid that the blood ran down into his eye, and he could not see. He stopped blowing for an instant and brushed the fly away. A hammer came out this time; but the handle was a little too short.

The three treasures were now finished, and Loki left the dwarfs, naming a day for them to meet him in Asgard. He set out at once for the home of the sons of Ivaldi. One of these artists, Thiassi, who was as large as a giant, and who was said to have great skill as a magician, went with him to Asgard. The treasures made by the last-named artists were already in the possession of the god.

It was a fair morning in the beautiful city when the judgment was to be pronounced. Gladsheim glittered in the sun. Upon its marble walls were pictured the wonders of the nine worlds, and the mighty deeds of gods and heroes in the earliest times. Mimir's mysterious valley, Urd's pure fountain, Mount Hvergelmir with its ice-cold spring – all could be seen on those vast walls. And there, too, were Surt's fiery dales below the realms of Urd, the dark, misty regions of Niflheim and even the world of torture with its stagnant sea. In other pictures lived again the strange beings and huge, uncouth monsters of the ancient world.

The great hall of Gladsheim was to be the scene of the judgment. 'There was Odin's throne. Over it rose the arch of Bifröst, so like the real bridge that it sent forth fitful flames. Behind the throne was a golden tree, representing Yggdrasil, the World Tree. The trembling leaves flashed in the sunlight that streamed in through the eastern openings. Sif, with her golden hair, sat near a table in the centre of the hall. And upon the table lay Odin's spear and Freyr's ship, made by the sons of Ivaldi.

The hour had come, and all eyes were turned toward the wide door, as Loki entered, accompanied by the enormous Thiassi. Loki's eyes sparkled with malicious pleasure; and, after making his reverence to Odin, he began talking gaily with the other gods.

Thiassi came in awkwardly, as though unused to scenes of such grandeur and beauty. He saluted Odin and the greater gods, and then seated himself near Sif, who tried in vain to make him talk with her.

In a few moments, two diminutive figures appeared at the great entrance, and with them a large boar whose golden bristles dazzled the eyes. One of the dwarfs led the boar, while the other carried a small hammer. They paid their respects to Odin and the other gods in a peculiar, jerky manner, and then stood looking about with eager, inquisitive faces.

Odin rose, and said, in a deep voice, 'We are here to decide upon the comparative skill of two sets of artists. They are both very skilful, and we are indebted to both for many rare and valuable gifts. It will be a difficult task to judge rightly, and we regret that Loki has made a judgment necessary. He, however, has promised to forfeit his head to Sindri and his brothers should the decision be in their favour.'

He paused a moment, and all looked at Loki's head on which the stiff, red hair gleamed like fire; a smile lurked about his treacherous mouth, and his eyes twinkled.

Odin went on: 'Let Thiassi state the peculiar properties and special merits of his work and that of his brothers; and then Sindri shall follow him, and speak of his gifts.'

Thiassi rose up, a sullen, defiant look in his face; evidently he was forced to play a part ill-suited to him. Pointing to Sif, he said, 'There is Thor's wife; you can all see her golden hair; it needs no praise.' Taking up the spear that lay on the table, he went on, 'This is a good spear; it never misses the mark.'

He next took from the table what seemed to be a white napkin; but as he held it, it bloomed and spread, until a ship appeared that grew larger and larger while he talked. 'This ship is like no other,' he said; 'it can be made small enough to be carried in the pocket, or large enough to hold many men; it always has a fair wind.'

Thiassi did not raise his eyes as he talked, but uttered every sentence as though it cost him an effort, making long pauses between. When he had finished speaking, he put the ship – which again looked like a napkin – upon the table, and with a sigh of relief sat down.

Sindri then came forward, his small, bright eyes peering everywhere, and his face eager and excited. His brother stood by his side, watching him intently and imitating all his gestures. Sindri pointed to the boar, saying: 'This boar is worthy of higher praise than I can give him. You see how his golden bristles flash in the sunlight; but in the darkest night their brightness is the same. On this boar Freyr can ride through Niflheim itself and still have day; and so swift is he that Sleipnir with his eight legs cannot outrun him. He can fly through the air, or skim over the sea, as his rider wills.' As he said this, Sindri looked keenly at Thiassi, as though searching in his face for a look of conscious defeat.

He next drew from his bosom a ring,[12] and as he held it up in the sunlight, all could see the stones of many colours that sparkled in the setting of yellow gold. After gazing upon it for a moment as though fascinated by the beautiful object, Sindri spoke: 'Were this ring merely what it seems, it would need no words of mine; but it has a most marvellous property. Every ninth night, eight rings of equal size and beauty drop from it. There is not another

---

12. The ring Draupnir, said to represent fertility.

treasure like it in all the nine worlds!' And Sindri put the ring down slowly, as though loath to part with it.

He then took the hammer from his brother. As he raised it, that it might be seen by all, it grew larger and larger, until the strength of both dwarfs was needed merely to hold it upright on the floor. With a look of triumph, Sindri cried: 'This mighty hammer, called Mjöllnir, will be more useful to Thor when he meets the frost giants than his wife's golden hair! It will strike whatever it is aimed at, without fail, let the thing be large or small; and it will always return to the hand that flings it. Besides, it can be easily carried; for it can be made so small as to go into the pocket.' He glanced at Loki as he added, 'To be sure, the handle is a little too short.'

As Sindri finished speaking, he and his brother looked around exultingly. Thiassi's face was expressionless, except for a haughty curl of the lip.

After a short pause, Odin rose, saying, 'Let Sif come here, and let all the treasures be brought. We will examine them carefully and then pronounce our judgment.'

While the gods were examining and consulting, the dwarfs watched them intently, their quick glance going from one to another; but Thiassi sat motionless, his head buried in his hands, apparently half asleep.

After a long consultation, silence was commanded. As Odin rose, every eye was fastened upon him. 'It has been a hard task', he began, 'to decide between such wonderful and useful gifts; but the decision must be given. We consider that the gifts made by the dwarfs, Sindri and his brothers, surpass in some respects those made by the sons of Ivaldi.' Then, turning to Loki, he added, 'Loki, you have forfeited your head; defend yourself as best you can!'

LOKI MAKES TROUBLE BETWEEN THE ARTISTS AND THE GODS 87

As Odin pronounced the judgment, a look of disappointment came into Thiassi's countenance, followed by an expression of fierce hatred, and bitter words escaped through his closed teeth. But the faces of the two dwarfs beamed with triumph and delight.

Sindri instantly sprang towards Loki, crying: 'Your head belongs to me, you crafty god! Never again shall you turn yourself into a fly to spoil the work of Sindri! Your red hair will make bristles for my next boar!' He tried to seize Loki, while he drew from beneath his mantle a large knife.

The nimble god slipped from his grasp, however, and was instantly out of the hall and speeding like the wind over the plains of Ida.

Sindri called for help. Then Thor, laughing mightily at the frantic rage of the dwarf, took up his hammer, and cried in a voice of thunder, 'Come back, you coward, or I'll try my hammer on you! Remember, it always hits!' The sound of Thor's voice produced a quick effect upon the runaway. He stopped, and came slowly back to the palace.

'Try your wits, now your heels have failed you,' said Thor.

As the dwarf again approached Loki, prepared to cut off his head, the latter cried, 'The head is yours, but not the neck!' Sindri stopped, and looked questioningly at the gods.

And they all said, 'Loki is right! Not the neck!'

'I am cheated,' yelled the angry dwarf. And quickly seizing his brother's awl, he sprang toward Loki, and in an instant had sewed his lips together with a stout thread. Thereupon he and his brother left the hall. Thiassi was nowhere to be seen. He had disappeared while Sindri and Loki were disputing.

Well had Loki succeeded in stirring up jealousy and hatred where all had been peace and good-will. Thiassi had left the great palace, full of rage against the gods, and with plans for revenge already seething in his brain; while Sindri and his brother were equally angry at the loss of their wager and at the mirth of the gods at their expense. Besides, the bitterest jealousy was now aroused between the two sets of artists.

BALDR AND LOKI

as told by Mary Litchfield

None of the gods stood so high in the judgment hall of the dead as Baldr. While he was not famed as a fighter, or noted for his strength, his pure heart and righteous life made his judgment so clear that his decisions were absolutely just, and once spoken were never questioned.

Besides being a perfect judge, Baldr had other qualities that made everyone love him, even the strong and fierce. He was so full of kindness and sympathy that wherever he went the sun shone more brightly, and joy filled all hearts. From the first his life had been blameless, and his one aim had been to make others happy. The loveliness of his character was expressed in his face and in his form; he was the most beautiful of all the gods: indeed, they often called him Baldr the Beautiful; and in Midgard, men named the whitest flower they could find Baldr's brow.

But dearly loved as he was, Baldr had one deadly enemy – the false, vindictive Loki. Loki secretly hated all the gods, but none so much as Baldr. His fierce jealousy was stirred because Baldr held such a high place in Asgard. He hated him as the darkness hates the light, and as evil abhors good; and all his plots and schemes tended to one end – the destruction of this hated being. He had long hoped to bring about in some way the downfall of Odin and the ruin of Asgard; but first he would kill Baldr, for well he knew that nothing would cause such universal grief as his death.

BALDR'S DREAMS

as told by Mary Litchfield

Baldr, the beloved of the gods, had grown sad. His palace, the 'Hall-of-broad-shining-splendour'[13], no longer gave him pleasure, and Nanna, his wife, could not comfort him. His voice was not heard in the council hall of the gods. Finally, after suffering long in silence, he confided to Odin and Frigg the cause of his sorrow. Every night, for a long while, he had been tormented by dreams which told him that the day of his death was not far distant, that he must leave the home he loved so well, to dwell in the under-world, apart from all his brethren. This thought made him so sad that the most joyous sights and sounds could not drive away his melancholy.

Odin at once called a council of all the gods and goddesses, and after conferring together, they sent some of their number to consult wise giants and other beings who knew more of the future than they themselves knew. All said that Baldr must die.

Then it was determined that from every living creature, and from all plants and metals, the oath not to harm Baldr should be exacted. Frigg received their oaths; and for days Asgard was thronged with the multitude of beings who came to take the solemn oath; until, finally, all had sworn.

But even this did not satisfy Odin. He resolved to go to the lower world and there seek information about the fate of his son.

---

13. Breidablik

Sleipnir was saddled; and the All-Father took the same road that he had travelled when he visited the realms of Mimir in search of wisdom. Again he crossed the celestial bridge, going towards the north, and passed again the shining castle of Heimdall, the sleepless watchman. But this time Sleipnir bore him swiftly through the dark ice region and the gloomy land of the mountain giants.

As he was going toward the south, a dog met him, having come evidently from the cave near Mount Hvergelmir. The breast of the dog was bloody, and so were his throat and his lower jaw. He barked furiously at Odin, and howled long after he had passed; but the All-Father rode on, not heeding him.

In the eastern part of Mimir's realm, near the home of Delling, the elf of the dawn, Odin came to a dense forest[14] that he could not remember having seen before.

---

14. The forest and castle have been introduced into the Baldr myth on Rydberg's authority. Mimir saved some pure mortals at the time of an impending catastrophe, and placed them in this castle. Baldr came, after his death, and ruled over them. After the destruction of the world, at Ragnarök, Baldr was to rule, and these mortals, who had long served him, were to re-people the earth. These lines from 'The Lay of Vafthrüdnir' in *Saemund's Edda* refer to the subject:

> What mortals will live,
> when the great Fimbul-winter
> shall from men have passed?'
> Vafthrûdnir: 'Lîf and Lîfthrasir;
> but they will be concealed
> in Hoddmimir's holt.
> The morning dews
> they will have for food.
> From them shall men be born.

Yet the locality was familiar to him, and he knew that a little farther to the east was the grave of the Vala,[15] whom he wished to consult. After penetrating for a long distance into the silent depths of the wood, he came to a wall, higher than the one around Asgard.

However, Sleipnir was not daunted by this obstacle; and in an instant Odin found himself in a large garden, from the midst of which rose a castle of singular beauty. The doors stood hospitably open: evidently no enemies were anticipated in this charmed spot, protected by forest and wall. The All-Father dismounted and entered.

Tall men and fair women walked about the castle, or talked together in small groups; and there were preparations as for some honoured guest whose coming was expected. At the upper end of the hall was a throne of gold, and near it benches, strewn with rings and ornaments; while on the table the mead stood ready; but it was covered with a shield.

As Odin entered, a graceful youth came forward, saying reverently, 'Are you the good king, and the wise, that Mimir has long promised us? You see that everything is in readiness, and your subjects await you with impatience.'

And Odin answered, 'I am indeed the king of a fair realm, but not your king. What is the name of him who is to rule over you?'

And the youth replied, 'Mimir has not told us his name; but we know he is to come ere long; and he will be so noble and so pure that we shall all love him and serve him gladly.'

Odin sighed, thinking of Baldr. After talking a little with the

---

15. A prophetess.

inhabitants of the castle, the All-Father left them, and made his way out of the forest.

Upon reaching the grave of the Vala, Odin chanted a magic song, compelling her to rise and answer him. She rose, and with a deathlike voice, said, 'What man is this, to me unknown, who has for me increased an irksome course? I have with snow been decked, by rain beaten and with dew moistened; long have I been dead.'

Odin did not give his real name, but said, 'Vegtam is my name; I am Valtam's son. Tell me what I wish to know of the realms of death; from earth I call on you. For whom are those benches strewn o'er with rings, and those costly couches o'erlaid with gold?'

And the Vala answered, 'Mead stands for Baldr brewed; over the bright potion a shield is laid; but the Æsir race are in despair. By compulsion I have spoken; I will now be silent.'

Then Odin spoke again: 'Be not silent, Vala; I will question you until I know all. I must yet know who will Baldr's slayer be; who will kill the son of Odin?'

The Vala said, 'Hödur[16] will thither his glorious brother send; he will the slayer of Baldr be; he will kill the son of Odin. By compulsion I have spoken; I will now be silent.'

However, Odin kept on questioning the Vala, until he asked something that revealed his true character; and she said, 'Not Vegtam are you, as I before believed; you are Odin, lord of men! Homeward ride, Odin, and exult! Nevermore shall man thus visit me, until Ragnarök, the Twilight of the Gods, has come.'

---

16. Said to be blind. He may have represented winter, the slayer of summer.

As she said this, the Vala sank back into the earth. And Odin rode again to Asgard, little comforted by what he had learned in the lower world.

THE MISTLETOE

as told by Abbie Farewell Brown

It seemed as though death could not come near Baldr now; for all beings had sworn that they would not hurt him. The purest of the gods was surely saved. One day he chanced to be hit by an arrow; and, had another been in his place, the wound would have been fatal; but when the arrow touched him, it was blunted, and he was not hurt. Seeing this, some of the gods begged him to stand as a mark, while they amused themselves by hurling things at him; stones, spears, arrows and swords – nothing could harm him.

Loki passed by as the Æsir were enjoying this game, and fierce jealousy filled his heart when he saw Baldr so calm in a position that would have meant death to any other being. Taking the form of a decrepit old woman, Loki went to the mansion of Frigg, and asked alms. Frigg gave the seeming beggar something, and then asked what the gods were doing as she crossed the plains of Ida. The woman replied that they were throwing stones and weapons at Baldr, who stood there, unhurt.

'Ah!' exclaimed the queen. 'They cannot harm him now, whatever his dreams may be, for I have exacted an oath from all things!'

'What!' said the woman, in a weak, shaky voice. 'Have all things sworn not to harm him?'

'Yes,' replied Frigg; 'all things.' Then she added carelessly, 'There was one little shrub, the mistletoe, that grows on the eastern side of Valhalla, too weak to do any harm. I did not exact an oath from that.'

Had Frigg been watching the old woman narrowly, she would have seen a look of triumph come into her face as she heard these words. But the queen of the gods scarcely noticed her, so absorbed was she in thinking of her dear son. And the beggar crept quietly out of the palace, and disappeared behind a clump of bushes.

In a few moments Loki was talking gaily with the gods on the plains of Ida, and congratulating Baldr on his ability to stand unhurt amid a shower of weapons.

After dark, when all Asgard was asleep, a form might have been seen creeping stealthily towards the eastern side of Valhalla. It was Loki. When he found the slender mistletoe, he pulled it up by the roots and hid it in his bosom. From that time it never left him; and he was continually planning to get some skilful maker of weapons to form from it an arrow fatal to Baldr.

THOR AND THRYM

as told by Mary Litchfield

Thor and Loki went to Jötunheim, in search of adventures. On the way home, night overtook them, and they lay down and slept on the edge of a forest. When Thor awoke, he felt for his hammer, and it was gone. His wrath was terrible. His fiery eyes and beard darted forth lightnings, and he struck his forehead as though he would awaken from a dream.

'Loki! Loki!' he cried. 'Awake! Hear what I tell you! No one on earth or in heaven knows this! The Æsir's hammer is stolen!'

Loki's face showed surprise and bewilderment. 'Stolen!' he replied. 'Your hammer? That cannot be!'

Then they looked all about them in the grass; but no hammer could be found. 'Thor,' said Loki, 'if I had Freyja's feather garment, I might find out where the hammer is. Do you think she would lend it to me?'

'The hammer must be found,' said Thor; 'if not, the giants of Jötunheim may prevail against us. Freyja will not refuse to help me.'

Very early in the morning they entered the city and went to Freyja's palace. Many warriors feasted there each day – mortals who had died on the field of battle, and lovers who had been faithful unto death.

As they entered the wide hall, Freyja rose to greet them. And seeing that Thor's brow was dark, she said, 'What ails you, Asa-Thor? Some trouble is surely in your heart!'

And Thor answered, 'The hammer, Mjöllnir, is stolen; it is in the hands of our enemies!'

'Mjöllnir stolen!' cried Freyja. 'How can that be? Who could take the hammer from mighty Thor?'

'I slept,' said Thor, 'and when I awoke, the hammer was gone. I can tell you no more.'

Freyja knew well what this meant. She pondered a moment, and then said, 'How can I help you, Thor?'

'Will you lend me your feather garment?' said Thor. 'With the help of that, the hammer may be found.'

'I would give it to you if it were made of gold, and trust it to you if it were of silver,' replied Freyja.

Thor and Loki left Freyja's palace, taking with them the feather garment. When they had gone a little way, they stopped, and Loki put on the plumage and flew towards Jötunheim. He flew so swiftly that the plumage rattled.

When he reached the icy land, he saw Thrym, the Thursar's lord, sitting on a mound, plaiting gold bands for his greyhounds, and smoothing his horses' manes. He knew Loki in spite of his disguise, and said, 'How are the Æsir getting on? And the elves? Why have you come alone to Jötunheim?'

'The Æsir are in a bad plight; and so are the elves,' Loki replied. 'Where have you hidden Thor's hammer?'

Thrym laughed aloud, and said, 'I have hidden Thor's hammer eight miles beneath the earth; and no man shall get it again unless he brings me Freyja for my wife.'

When Loki heard this, he too laughed; for he was not sorry that Thor had lost his hammer.

He flew back to Asgard in the rattling plumage.

When he came near to Thor's palace, the latter saw him, and

called out, 'Have you had success as well as labour? Tell me your story from the air. The man who sits down leaves out too much; and he who lies down speaks falsely.'

Loki answered from the air: 'I have had labour and success. Thrym, the Thursar's lord, has your hammer. And no man can get it again unless he bring him Freyja for his wife.' Then Loki flew to the ground and took off the feather garment; and he and Thor went to Freyja's palace.

When Freyja saw them, she welcomed them. Glad was she to get her falcon plumage again. But Thor's brow was dark, and he said, 'Put on your bridal garments, Freyja; for we two must drive to Jötunheim.'

Freyja did not understand him. So he told her that unless she became the wife of the giant Thrym, Mjöllnir would never be returned.

'Make ready, therefore, and come with me!' said Thor. 'Or the giants will storm Asgard; and without the hammer, who can defend it against them?'

Freyja grew very angry as Thor talked. She was a mighty goddess, tall and powerful. And as her anger raged, the hall where they were trembled, and the great Brisinga[17] necklace shivered into pieces. 'Never will I drive with you to Jötunheim!' cried Freyja. 'Never will I be the bride of Thrym!'

Thor and Loki left the palace, and sought Odin, the wise All-Father. As soon as Odin heard what had happened, he called a council of all the gods and goddesses; for the safety of Asgard

---

17. A famous necklace made by the dwarfs.

depended upon their getting back Thor's hammer.

The council met. When many had spoken to no purpose, Heimdall arose. He had the wisdom of the Vanir.

'I think I know how we may get back the hammer,' he said. 'Let Thor be clothed in Freyja's garments; let keys jingle at his side; place precious stones on his breast; around his neck put the famed Brisinga necklace; and set a neat coif[18] on his head. Clad thus, he may deceive the giant, and get again the mighty hammer, Mjöllnir.'

These words did not please Thor. He said, 'The Æsir will call me womanish if I let myself be clad in bridal raiment.'

Loki rejoiced secretly at the thought of Thor in a woman's robes, and he said, 'Speak not such words, Thor! The giants will soon rule in Asgard if you do not get back Mjöllnir.'

The Æsir all agreed that Heimdall's words were wise. And after much urging, Thor allowed them to clothe him in Freyja's garments. They put the famed Brisinga necklace around his neck; keys jingled at his side; precious stones sparkled upon his breast; and on his head was a neat coif.

Loki was delighted, and he said to Thor, 'I will go as your serving-maid; we two will drive to Jötunheim together.'

The goats were found in their rocky pastures. They were quickly driven home, and hurried into the traces; and Thor and Loki leaped into the chariot. Like mountain winds let loose the goats sped on. The rocks were shivered, and the earth was in a

---

18. A kind of cap.

blaze; for the mighty thunder-god drove in his wrath to Jötunheim.

When Thrym, the Thursar's lord, saw them coming, he was glad; for he thought the desire of his heart was won – Freyja was to be his wife.

'Rise up, Jötuns!' he cried. 'And deck the benches; for they bring Freyja, Njörd's daughter, from Noatûn, to be my wife. Bring hither gold-horned cows and all-black oxen for the joy of the Jotuns. I had many necklaces and many treasures; but Freyja I lacked. With her I shall want nothing.'

Early in the evening, many giants came to the wedding feast; and much beer was brought out for them. Thor alone devoured an ox and eight salmon, and all the sweetmeats women like. He also drank three barrels of mead.

Thrym, the king of the giants, was astonished to see a woman eat so much, and he said, 'Did you ever see such a hungry bride? I never saw a bride eat so much, nor a maiden drink so much mead!'

The crafty serving-maid sat close by, and she found a ready answer. She said to the Jötun, 'For eight days Freyja has eaten nothing, she has longed so for Jötunheim.'

Then the giant stooped to kiss the bride under her veil; but he suddenly sprang back, saying, 'Why are Freyja's looks so piercing? Methinks fire comes from her eyes.'

The crafty serving-maid found again fitting words.

'Well may her eyes be piercing; Freyja did not sleep for eight nights, so eager was she for Jötunheim.'

The sister of the giant then came in. She, luckless woman, dared ask for a bride-gift. 'Give me the ruddy rings from your hands,' she said, 'if you would gain my friendship and my love.'

Thrym, the Thursar's lord, then said: 'Bring in the hammer to consecrate the bride. Lay Mjöllnir on the maiden's knees. Unite us with each other in the name of Var.'[19]

When he saw the hammer, Thor's heart leaped within him. Fierce joy filled his soul at the sight of Mjöllnir. He rose in his might and slew Thrym, the Thursar's lord, and crushed all the race of giants. Last of all he slew the giant's aged sister. For a bridal gift she got the stroke of Mjöllnir – blows of the hammer instead of many rings.

Thus did Odin's son get back his mighty hammer.

---

19. Var or Vor, the goddess of betrothals and marriages.

THOR AND SKRYMIR

as told by Mary Litchfield

Thor sat in his great palace, of which Odin said, 'Five hundred floors, and forty eke, I think, has Bilskirnir, with its windings. Of all the roofed houses that I know, is my son's the greatest.' The thunder-god was uneasy; for his fierce, restless spirit could never be satisfied unless warring against the giants or seeking adventures in some distant land. He went from one hall to another, and at last, with a sigh, threw himself upon a couch that was covered with the skin of a wild beast. His powerful frame showed the muscles of an athlete, and his red beard gleamed like fire.

The walls of the hall where he lay were thickly hung with shields of rare workmanship, and between them were spears and swords that flashed in the sunlight. But the glories of his great palace had no charm for Thor now; he yawned, and cast wistful glances towards the north, as though he could discern even at that distance the dreary mountains of his foes.

Suddenly a form darkened the doorway, and Loki stood before him. The thunder-god did not like Loki; he distrusted him. The love of adventure was so strong in both, however, that it sometimes drew them together.

'Thor,' said Loki, as he entered, 'order your chariot, and let us drive to Jötunheim. Asgard may do for Baldr, but I am tired of it; I long for something new.'

Fire flashed from Thor's listless eyes; and he sprang up, saying, 'Well spoken, Loki! Get ready; we will go at once.'

They started off towards the north in Thor's heavy, rumbling chariot, drawn by the famous goats. Thor had with him three things that he never meant to leave behind: the hammer, Mjöllnir, which always returned to him when he flung it, and never missed the mark; the iron gloves which enabled him to grasp the hammer more firmly; and the belt of power.

They journeyed all day over barren fields and plains, and as night fell, found themselves in an almost uninhabited country. A tiny house standing on the edge of a forest was the only dwelling in sight. As they came near, some heads appeared at the doorway and suddenly disappeared. Evidently the inmates were frightened: and well they might be; for the rumbling of Thor's iron chariot sounded like thunder, and his red beard and fiery eyes flashed so in the gathering darkness that they might have been mistaken for lightning.

Thor was about to drive on, not heeding the house, when Loki cried imploringly: 'Do stop, I pray you, Thor! With your great strength you forget that ordinary gods may get tired and hungry after rattling about in your chariot all day with nothing to eat!'

Thor laughed heartily, and said: 'I forgot who was with me; Loki and food may not long be parted. This is a small house, but it may give us food and shelter.'

They alighted from the chariot and went in. The peasants cowered in one corner of the room, on seeing the wonderful strangers, so tall that they could not stand upright in the small house.

Loki spoke: 'Do not be frightened, good people. We are hungry travellers who desire rest and food. We will not harm you, but will reward you generously for your hospitality.'

Reassured by Loki's mild words, and Thor's good-natured smile, they came forward, still trembling. The woman made a deep curtsey, and said: 'My good lords, we welcome you, and would gladly give you some supper; but the little food we had is eaten, and there is nothing left in the house; we are very poor.'

'Never mind,' said Thor; 'do as I bid you, and I will manage the rest.' Then, turning to the man, he said, 'Go and unharness my goats, while your wife makes the fire and gets the pot ready; we will cook some meat.'

The peasants did as Thor bade them, though they could not imagine where the meat was coming from.

Loki helped the woman make the fire, while Thor followed the man out. As soon as the goats were unharnessed, he knocked them both on the head with his hammer, and told the peasant to prepare them for cooking. Soon an enormous platter of goats' flesh was smoking on the table.

As Thor helped the peasants and their two children to the meat, he said: 'Eat all you will, good people, but beware of breaking the bones. I have a special reason for wishing them to be kept whole.'

Thialfi, the son, had rarely tasted meat, so this was a great feast for him. As he was picking the meat from one of the thigh-bones, Loki whispered, 'The marrow inside the bone is best of all!' and Thialfi, forgetting Thor's command, cracked the bone and sucked out the marrow.

Raska, his sister, ate but little. She spent her time in gazing with open-mouthed wonder at the tall strangers who ate with such evident relish the goats that served them as horses. And she asked herself what they would do on the morrow, with the heavy iron chariot, and no goats to draw it.

After the hearty meal all were soon fast asleep.

Thor awoke as the first rays of the early dawn shot into the little room. Jumping up quickly, he gathered together the bones of the goats and put them into the skins. Then lifting his mighty hammer, he repeated some magic words, called runes. Instantly the two goats were skipping about as lively as if they had enjoyed a good meal and a night's rest instead of having served as food for others; but Thor noticed that one of them limped. Suspecting the cause, he became furious with anger, and called out in a loud voice, 'Wake up, you wretched peasants! See what you have done to my goats!'

The peasants started as though waked by a thunder-clap, and cowered, trembling, before the angry god.

'Who broke the thigh-bone of my goat?' roared Thor, clutching Mjöllnir till his knuckles grew white, while flashes of light came from his eyes and beard, threatening to burn the room.

Then Thialfi, who was a brave lad, plucked up his courage, and said: 'Oh! Mighty sir, I broke the thigh-bone of your goat. I forgot what you said; the meat was so good; and I wanted to get the marrow. Punish me, but do not harm the others; they have done nothing.'

The boy's courage and honesty touched Thor, who was really kind at heart. And he said: 'You have done a very bad deed, but I will forgive you, because you are brave and speak the truth. A liar and a coward I cannot abide. But you are too good a fellow to spend your life in this hut like a beast. Come with me, and you shall see the world. Your sister shall come too. You shall live in a big house. If this little hut were put into it, you might hunt all day and not find it.'

Then Thor gave the peasant and his wife a handful of gold, saying, 'Your children shall come and see you when they will.' And when they were starting off, he said, 'I leave the goats and

the chariot in your care until my return. Do not break any bones!'
And he laughed heartily.

So the four started into the thick forest. Thialfi, who was very fleet of foot, carried the bag containing food for the journey; and Raska, who was a stout peasant-girl, kept up easily with the others. After a long walk through the forest, they came to the great river, Ocean, on the other side of which lay Jötunheim. They crossed the sea without much trouble, although it was a long distance over it.

On the other side was a land much wilder than the one they left behind. Everything was enormous in size; the stones being as large as rocks, and the trees reaching to the clouds. After crossing a barren stretch of country, strewn with huge boulders, they came to a deep forest where perfect silence reigned, and where there was nothing green underfoot, for the ground was covered with pine-needles. It was like twilight in this forest even at noon, the thick branches let so little sunlight through; and besides, the sun never shone brightly in any part of Jötunheim.

All day they travelled on, and one part of the wood was so exactly like another that they might have gone about in a circle had not Thialfi now and then climbed to the top of a tall tree to make sure that they were going in the right direction.

As night fell, the little light that filtered through the branches faded away, leaving them in utter darkness. It was impossible to go on without running against the trees. Thor, impatient as he was to proceed, decided to stop and wait for the morning. In the darkness they felt around for a good place to sleep. As Loki was groping about, he touched something that was not a tree; and, as he ran his hand up, it seemed like the entrance to a house.

'This is very strange!' he exclaimed. 'Strike a light, Thialfi! Here is some kind of a house, but whoever lives in it must be fond of the woods!'

Thialfi did as Loki requested, and by the flaring light of a dry stick they could distinguish a large opening. A dwelling of some kind it was, certainly, but of a new pattern; for the door was the size of the whole front of the house.

'There's nothing like travelling to see strange sights!' said Loki. And as they went in, he remarked, 'This house is of an odd shape, but it seems to be a good place to sleep in.'

They threw themselves down on the floor of the large entrance hall, and were soon fast asleep.

About midnight they were awakened by a terrible shaking of the earth, together with a rumbling noise like thunder. They started up, expecting to feel another shock in a moment, for apparently it was an earthquake. But all was still. Thor placed himself in the main door of the house, while the others found some smaller rooms that promised greater quiet.

As soon as the first rays of the sun struggled through the branches, so that Thor could distinguish one object from another, he fastened on his belt of strength, drew on his iron gauntlets and, grasping his hammer firmly, strode out into the forest to seek the cause of the noise and the shaking that had so disturbed their slumbers. He expected to find a mighty chasm yawning nearby – the result of the earthquake.

He had not gone far, when he saw a hill rising in an opening amid the trees; and at the same time he heard a loud sound that evidently came from the further side of the hill. When Thor reached that side, he could just distinguish in the dim light the enormous head of a giant from whose open mouth came the sounds he had heard. What Thor had taken for a hill was the giant's body. His eyes were closed, and his eyebrows stood out like lines of bushes from above them. His hair looked more like a forest of trees than like the hair of a common person.

Thor looked at the sleeping giant for a moment and then aimed his hammer at his forehead. But instead of flinging it, he stopped short, and reaching up, put his mouth near his ear, and roared in a voice of thunder, 'What is your name?'

The giant stretched his huge limbs, and slowly opened his eyes. At first he seemed dazed; but gradually a look of intelligence came into his face, and he said, slowly, 'Did anybody speak?'

'Yes,' roared Thor, 'I did. What's your name?'

As the giant heard Thor's voice, he turned his large head slowly around and looked at him. After a long stare, he replied, 'Skrymir.' Then he added, 'I know you; you are Asa-Thor.'

'You had better thank me,' said Thor; 'I seldom begin my acquaintance with giants in so polite a manner, as some of your friends have learned to their cost.'

Skrymir smiled, but it took a good while. After another pause he broke the silence with, 'What have you done with my glove?' And he slowly stretched out his hand and picked up the house where they had spent the night. Luckily Loki and the others had just left it. There was a look of amusement on Skrymir's enormous features that irritated Thor greatly; but he tried to look unconcerned.

At last the giant got up, shook his huge limbs, and said, good-naturedly: 'Will you little people accept of the company of such a large person as myself? I should like to join you; and we may be useful to one another, although we differ in size.'

Thor accepted Skrymir's offer, but his words angered him so that he clutched Mjöllnir. The giant next untied an immense provision sack in which he carried his food, and began to eat his breakfast. Thor, who could enjoy the society of giants only when he was fighting them, went off to a little distance and ate with his companions.

As they were finishing their meal, the giant came crashing through the woods to where they were, and said: 'Here, friends, I am big, and you are small. Put your provisions into my sack. I can carry everything easily.'

There was no reason for refusing the offer of the good-natured giant, so they put all the food into his sack. He flung the bag over his shoulder, and led the way with long strides.

It was a hard day's journey. But Thor was too proud to own that they could not easily keep up with a giant; so instead of asking him to slacken his pace, they ran all the way.

Toward night, Skrymir stopped under a large oak. Flinging himself down, he handed the provision sack to Thor, saying, 'Here, Asa-Thor, take this. I am more sleepy than hungry, and do not care for food.' In an instant he was sound asleep, and snoring so loudly that the woods resounded and the earth trembled.

Thor took the bag and started to untie the strings; but with all his efforts not a knot would come undone, nor could he even loosen one. At this his blood began to boil; and seizing Mjöllnir, he flung it with all his might at the head of the sleeping giant.

Skrymir stirred a little, put his hand to his head, and slowly opened his large blue eyes, saying, 'Did a leaf fall on my head? I thought I felt something.' Then looking at Thor, he asked, 'Have you eaten your supper yet? Aren't you going to bed?'

'Yes,' replied Thor; 'we are going to bed.' And as he would not ask Skrymir to untie the sack, they lay down, hungry and tired, under a tree, not very far from the giant.

Skrymir made such a roaring that it was almost impossible to sleep. As Thor lay there, hearing the dreadful noise, he grew more and more furious. At last he started up with an oath, and going to where the giant lay, swung Mjöllnir with all his Asa-might, and plunged it into his forehead up to the handle.

The giant stopped snoring, and turning uneasily, muttered, 'What is the matter now? Did an acorn fall upon my forehead? Where are you, Thor?'

Then, with a sigh, he was fast asleep again, and snoring as loudly as ever.

Thor was by this time so angry that, even had all been quiet, he could not have slept. He sat for hours leaning against the tree, his comrades asleep near him. Instead of growing calmer, he grew more enraged as the hours went by.

When the morning light showed again the outlines of the giant's huge form, he went over to where he lay. This time he swung Mjöllnir as he had never swung it before, and buried it so deeply in the giant's temple that only a little of the handle stuck out. 'Can you feel that?' he roared.

Skrymir opened his eyes, and as they rested upon the angry god, asked sleepily: 'Are there any birds on the tree above me? I thought some moss fell upon my forehead.' Then opening his eyes wider, he added, 'But it is morning, and we must start on.'

When they were ready to go, the giant turned to Thor with an odd smile on his face, and said, 'You evidently think me rather large, Asa-Thor; but when you reach Utgard, you will find larger men than I. Let me give you some advice: do not brag too much. Utgard-Loki, the lord of Utgard, and his big courtiers will not stand the boasting of little men like you. In fact, the best thing you can do is to turn back and give up visiting Utgard. Dangers that you little suspect may lie before you in that giant-land.'

Thor tried to answer Skrymir, but he was so choked with rage that the words would not come out.

The giant continued, 'If you are determined to go on, turn to the east, toward the mountains that you see yonder."' And taking the provision sack, he disappeared in the woods.

Thor started after him with Mjöllnir; but he seemed to have changed suddenly into a large grey mountain on their right.

As the giant had carried off the food, they were forced to content themselves with the few berries and roots that they could find on their way; for there was no game in the woods.

About noon the forest ended abruptly, and they came into a large plain that extended on all sides like a grey sea. There were rocks here and there; but not a blade of grass, not a tree gladdened the eye as it roamed over the dreary waste. In the midst of the plain was a huge castle. Even at that distance they had to bend back their necks in order to see its turrets, half hidden by clouds. It looked as though carved roughly by giants out of a rocky mountain. Its rude walls bore the scars of time, and showed in places the fierce sport of the lightning.

Thor and his companions went towards the castle, clambering over the boulders. It was farther off than they had thought: its great size made it seem near.

When at last they stood before the high walls that surrounded it, night was beginning to fall. The great god Thor seemed but a child as he stretched up his hand to reach the lock of the ponderous gate. In vain: it was too high for him. Loki had already wriggled between the bars; and he now called to the others to follow him. Once inside the walls, they saw through the open door of the castle a hall larger than Thor's whole palace.

The gods and their companions walked in boldly and looked about. They could see clouds floating in and out through jagged openings in the vast heights above. In the centre of the hall was a table of rough granite which was supported by monsters whose wide-open jaws made huge caverns. At the upper end of the table was Utgard-Loki, the giant-king. He sat on a high seat, the back and arms of which were formed by the coils of the Midgard serpent sculptured in stone. The huge, horrid head of the monster stretched out over the king. The beard of Utgard-Loki was the colour of the grey rocks, and fell in masses to the ground. His motions were heavy and slow. When he reached his hand for the beer-mug which stood near him on the table, it was some time before it reached his lips; and after a long drink he would give a sigh of satisfaction that sounded like the roaring of the wind. His features were slow in changing their expression. His large round eyes were neither kind nor fierce; for they had no more human feeling in them than cold mountain lakes.

On each side of the table there were stone benches whose high backs made comfortable resting-places for the heads of the giants. These giants were nearly as large as Utgard-Loki, and all were drinking beer. Someone had evidently made a joke just before Thor and his companions entered; for a deep, slow 'Ha! Ha!' came from one and then another of the giants, until the roar of their great guffaws filled the vast hall, and rolled out like thunder into the gathering night. The gods could examine everything at their leisure; for not one of the giants seemed aware of their presence.

Thor's blood began to boil as he looked at the dull, mountain-like creatures; and he longed to fling his hammer and change them into real mountains as they sat on their benches of stone; but he forbore, and going up to Utgard-Loki, placed himself directly in front of him. The king turned his expressionless eyes upon him, and after staring for several moments, burst into a loud laugh, showing his granite teeth.

'Why, what have I before me?' he roared. 'This stripling must be Asa-Thor of whom I have often heard. I am surprised! But perhaps you are really bigger than you look!' Then in a moment he added: 'What can you do? We always make our guests prove their strength or their skill before we invite them to eat and drink with us.'

Loki was very hungry, and pushing himself in front of Thor, he cried eagerly, 'I will wager that no one here can eat as fast as I can!' And he laughed to himself at the thought of contending with the slow, clumsy giants.

Then Utgard beckoned to a man that Loki had not noticed. He sat at the lower end of the table, and was small and agile compared with the giants. A trough full of meat was brought in.

'Logi,' said the king, 'show this little man that giants can be as quick as he.'

They began to eat, seated at opposite ends of the trough. Loki ate ravenously; for pride and hunger both spurred him on. Neither stopped to look at the other, till at last they met in the very middle of the trough. Loki then saw, to his amazement, that while he had eaten all the meat on his side, Logi had consumed not only the meat but the bones, and even the trough itself. So there was no question as to who had won the victory. However, the fact that he had enjoyed a hearty meal consoled Loki in part for his defeat.

Utgard next turned his eyes to where Thialfi stood and, pointing at him with his huge forefinger, asked, 'What can that young man do?'

Thialfi straightened up, and answered proudly: 'I can run a race with anyone you may appoint. He must be swifter than the eagle if he can outrun me!' The king rose slowly from his seat and walked with a lumbering gait through the vast hall and out upon the plain surrounding the castle. A few giants followed, one after another, and seated themselves on the large boulders that lay around.

Utgard-Loki pointed out the course, and then called in a loud voice, 'Hugi, come here!'

Quick as a flash appeared an agile little fellow, apparently more akin to the elves than to the giants. A peculiar, dull smile overspread the features of the king as he said, 'We do not match you little people against our giants; that would be hardly fair; this is one of our dwarfs.' And he and his courtiers laughed loud and long at the joke.

The course pointed out was a long one, but Thialfi started like a steed of high mettle eager for the race. He flew as the swallow flies. Yet Hugi was so much swifter that he touched the goal and met Thialfi on the return before the latter had finished the course.

Utgard-Loki laughed, saying, 'You must ply your legs better, little Thialfi; though you are a very fair runner!'

They ran a second time; and when Hugi turned back from the goal, Thialfi was a good bow-shot from it.

'Well run, Thialfi!' cried the king of the giants. 'No better runner has ever visited us; but, for once, you have evidently found your match. One more course shall decide the contest.'

This time Thialfi sped as swiftly as the winds that rush over the open plain; one could hardly see him as he flew along. Yet still his rival outstripped him; and when they met, Thialfi was not half-way to the goal. Even Thor cried out that it was enough. And eager to show that he, at least, could outdo the giants, he demanded a trial of his powers.

'Let me show your courtiers how an Asa can drink!' he said. 'I do not fear to contend with the mightiest of you!'

They returned to the hall; and Utgard-Loki, again seating himself on his high throne, called out to his cup-bearer, 'Bring hither our ancient drinking-horn!' Then he explained to Thor that it was from this horn that his courtiers were obliged to drink when they had trespassed in any way against the established usage of the land.

When the cup-bearer brought the horn, Thor found that while it was not very large at the top, it was exceedingly long, winding in coil after coil, so that it was hard to distinguish the end. Indeed, it reached far across the hall, and was there lost in the shadows. Thor gazed at it with interest. He saw that strange sea-monsters were carved upon it, and that its coils were encrusted with shells and barnacles, and fringed with sea-mosses.

The god was very thirsty, and with an expression of satisfaction he raised the horn to his lips. Long and deep was his draught. As he drank, the sound was like that of water breaking upon a pebbly beach. Yet when he stopped, breathless, and looked to see how much beer was left in the horn, he found, to his surprise, that there was about as much as at first.

Raising the horn again, he drank as long as he could without taking breath, and then looked in. The liquor had sunk even less than before.

Utgard-Loki smiled broadly, and said, 'How now, Thor! Have you not saved for the third draught more than you can make away with? You must not spare yourself too much in a test of this kind. If you wish to drain the horn, you must drink deep!'

Thor was in a towering passion as he raised the horn for the third time. It seemed as though he would never stop drinking. The noise he made was like the roar of the waves as they dash upon the rocks in a storm; and yet, when he stopped and looked at the horn, the liquor was so high that it could only just be carried without spilling.

Shame and anger were pictured on Thor's face as he gave back the horn to the cup-bearer. 'I own myself beaten,' he said; 'but let me try something else: I know I can outdo you giants in something.'

'There is a little game our children sometimes play,' said the king; 'supposing you try that. I would not propose a child's game to Thor, had he not shown himself much weaker than I thought him. See if you can lift my cat from the ground.'

As he was speaking, a large grey cat ran across the hall. Thor sprang towards her, and putting his hand under her body, tried to lift her from the ground; but as he raised his hand, she curved her back, and with his utmost efforts he could only raise one foot from the floor.

'Just as I expected,' said Utgard-Loki; 'the cat is large, and Thor is small compared with our men.'

'You call me small,' cried Thor, thoroughly enraged; 'but which of you dares wrestle with me now that I am angry? 'and his eyes darted forth sparks, and from his beard shot flames of fire, lighting up the grey hall.

'I see no one here', said the king, looking around, 'who would not think it beneath him to wrestle with a little man like you. But here comes my old nurse Elli; she has thrown to the ground many a man as strong and boastful as Thor.'

An old woman, bent nearly double, came into the hall. She was toothless, and had scant, grey locks. Her thin form trembled as she raised her bleared and almost sightless eyes to Thor. He looked at her with disgust.

'Wrestle with him, mother,' said Utgard-Loki.

Whereupon she wound her long, thin arms about Thor, and the more he tried to throw her, the more firmly did she stand. At last, worn out with the conflict, the god sank upon one knee.

The king then stepped forward and said it was enough. Then he added, 'Although you little people have shown yourselves weak compared with us giants, still we admire your spirit, and we invite you to eat and drink with us.'

Thor and his companions were by this time thoroughly vexed and humbled. They gave up the contest, and accepted the hospitality of Utgard-Loki.

Long was the feast, and strange and dull were the stories told by the giants as they nodded over the foaming beer. Thor, as he sat in the dreary stone hall, thought of the wit and gaiety that reigned in Gladsheim. But the giants seemed to be enjoying themselves.

The gods awoke at daybreak, and Utgard-Loki went with them through the iron gate. When on the other side he said: 'What do you think of your journey, Asa-Thor? Do you consider that you have met your match among the giants this time?'

'I own myself beaten,' said Thor; 'I am ashamed. It vexes me to think in what esteem you must hold me.'

'Well, Asa-Thor,' replied the giant, 'since you are beyond my castle walls, I will tell you the truth, if it will be any comfort to you. And first, let me say, that never again shall you or any Asa enter within my walls!

'I have all along deceived you by enchantments. It was I who met you in the forest, and there I found out how strong you were. The provision sack which you tried in vain to untie was fastened with iron; that was why you could not open it. The blows of your hammer were so mighty that the first one would have killed me had I not, by magic, brought a mountain between us. On your return you will see a mountain with three square glens, each deeper than the one before it. Those are the marks left by your hammer.

'In the same way I deceived you in your contests with my courtiers. Loki ate like hunger itself; but Logi was wild-fire, and that consumes all that is set before it. Thialfi's running struck us all with amazement, for he outstripped the wind; but Hugi was my thought, and that can fly more swiftly than the lightning as it flashes from peak to peak.

When you tried to empty our ancient horn, you performed a feat so marvellous that had I not seen it myself I should never have believed it. The end of the horn, which you could not see, reached to the ocean. You drank so deeply that you lowered the great river. When you reach it on your way home, you will see how the water has fallen. In Midgard they will henceforth call this the ebb.

When you lifted from the ground one paw of my cat, you were in reality raising the great Midgard serpent that encircles the earth. And you lifted him so high that you nearly pulled his tail out of his mouth. We feared the foundations of Jötunheim would be shaken. But your wrestling with Elli was the most astonishing feat of all. She was no other than old age. And there never has been, and never will be, a man whom old age cannot lay low, if he abide her coming. You are a mighty god, Asa-Thor, and I shall take good care that you never find my country again, however diligently you may seek for it. We giants, dull and heavy as we may seem, have the wisdom of the ages.'

Thor raised his hammer, but Utgard-Loki had vanished. And turning his eyes to where the castle was, he saw nothing but a beautiful green plain, upon which the slow-moving clouds cast their shadows.

Thor returned to his home in Asgard; but the memory of his adventures in the castle of Utgard-Loki stung him continually; and he determined to revenge himself by attacking the Midgard serpent in his ocean home.

THOR'S JOURNEY TO GET THE KETTLE FOR ÆGIR

as told by Mary Litchfield

Ægir, the ruler of the stormy western sea, feasted all the gods at harvest time; but there was never quite enough beer to go round. This angered Thor, for it showed a lack of hospitality; and he told Ægir, very bluntly, what he thought of it.

Ægir appeared to feel hurt, and said: 'Your words are rude and unkind, Asa-Thor; the reason why the beer does not hold out is that I have no kettle large enough for the brewing. It is no small matter to make beer for all the dwellers in Asgard.'

Tyr, who stood near, turned to Thor, and said: 'My father, the fierce giant Hymir, dwells near heaven's end. He owns a caldron a mile deep. I think we can manage in some way to get it from him. Ægir will then have the satisfaction of entertaining his friends in a manner befitting his generous nature.'

'It is too bad to trouble you,' said Ægir; 'it is such a long journey, and you may not be able to get the caldron, after all.'

'Oh, friend Ægir!' cried Thor. 'We count nothing as trouble if it only obliges you. Come, Tyr, let us be off! My goats are ready, and I long to see Jötunheim again. If I can only meet the Midgard serpent on this journey, I will pay him well for deceiving me as he did at Utgard-Loki's – making me lift him for a cat!'

So the two gods started off together. Tyr was a more fit companion for Thor than Loki was. He was as fearless as the thunder-god himself, and one of the noblest of the Æsir.

Thor put up his goats at some distance from the giant's castle; for wherever he went in his great rumbling chariot he was known as the mighty god of thunder; and this time he wished to go quietly.

Night was coming on as they neared the dwelling of Hymir, which stood by the frozen shore, surrounded by rocks and icebergs. The sides of the huge castle glistened with frost, and from its projections hung long icicles. As they went in through the wide door, the first object to meet their eyes was a giantess with nine hundred heads. She was nodding sleepily with all her heads in a corner of the vast hall; and she did not notice them. This was Hymir's mother.

A great fire of pine and fir trees burned at one end of the room, and near it sat a lovely woman, the firelight shining on her golden-brown hair. She greeted her son and his friend joyfully, and brought beer to refresh them after their long journey. Then looking out into the night, she said: 'My husband will soon be home from his fishing. But he is often in an ill-humour, and the sight of guests might put him in a rage. Fearless as you are, do as I bid you: hide under those kettles at the other end of the room. It is dark there, and he will not see you.' They did as she bade them.

Before long there was a loud rushing and roaring sound; it was Hymir coming home from his fishing, wading through the sea. Great waves broke upon the rocks and icebergs; and the sound of the giant's breathing was like the roaring of winds. The earth trembled beneath his tread, and the walls of the castle were shaken. As he entered, the gods saw that his huge head glistened with ice and snow and that 'the thicket on his cheeks was frozen'. With a grunt of ill-humour he threw down his net in which were whales and other sea-monsters, not yet dead.

His wife rose up, trembling, to meet him, and spoke gently, saying: 'You must be tired, my husband, after your hard day's fishing. You see I have a good fire, and supper will soon be ready. It is a fierce night. Even you must have found it hard coming through the sea.' A rough growl was the only reply to her kind words.

After Hymir had sat by the fire some time, and had taken great draughts of hot beer, his wife spoke to him again, saying: 'I have been thinking much of our son Tyr of late; and, strange to say, he came home today; and he brought his friend Thor with him – Thor, the great thunder-god. I know you will be glad to see them.

'Where are they?' roared Hymir; and he glanced toward the dark end of the hall, where the kettles hung. The huge wooden beam broke as his eyes rested upon it, and eight kettles fell, all breaking but one. That one was the largest of all, a hard-hammered cauldron. The gods then stood forth, their shapely forms in strange contrast with the huge, uncouth figure of the giant. When Hymir saw the flashing of Thor's eyes, he felt that it boded evil to him.

Three oxen were cooked for supper, and Thor ate two of them. The giant, thinking such a guest would soon make havoc in his larder, said gruffly, 'We shall have to live on what we can catch in the sea, tomorrow!'

'Nothing would suit me better than to go fishing with you, giant Hymir,' said Thor.

The next morning the giant got ready for the expedition. Being in a bad humour, he said, 'Get your own bait if you are going with me! You can catch an ox for yourself.'

Thor found the herd of the giant, and going up to a coal-black bull, the finest of all, wrung his head from his neck and took it for bait.

When Hymir saw the head of his best bull, he said, 'I wish you had sat quiet, and had let me get the bait!'

They started out in Hymir's boat, both rowing. Thor's mighty strokes sent the boat scudding over the angry sea. When they were far out, the giant said: 'This is my fishing ground. Here I catch whales. We will stop.'

'It is child's play to fish so near the shore,' said Thor, redoubling the might of his strokes.

The sea grew rougher, and great waves broke over the boat. When at last they were in the very middle of the ocean, Thor stopped rowing. The giant at once threw his line, and drew up two whales with one bait.

Then Thor took out a line, which although slender was of great strength. He fastened the gory head of the black ox firmly to the hook. Down, down went the bait, far below the rough waves; deeper than where the whales sported; down to the very bottom of the ocean. There lay the mighty earth-encircler, the giant serpent of the deep.[20] For years he had lain in the quiet of the deep sea, with his tail down his throat, waiting with slow-burning hatred for the time of vengeance, the Twilight of the Gods. The coils of his mighty body were fringed with sea-mosses, and covered with clinging shells. Tall sea-palms waved gently in the dim waters above his head. Never, in all the long years, had bait with hook come near his dull eyes.

---

20. See Oehlenschläger's poem, 'Thor's Fishing', in Longfellow's *Poets and Poetry of Europe*. The same poem may be found in Frye's translation of Oehlenschläger's *Gods of the North*.

Thor had secured a most tempting bait. The gory head of the ox came near the serpent's head, and then floated slowly away like a living thing. Then it came near again. A look of eagerness came into the serpent's cruel eyes, and he drew his tail slowly from his jaws. As it reached him the third time, he opened wide his jaws, snatched it, and swallowed head, hook and all. Then came the struggle.

Thor pulled with such strength that his feet broke through the bottom of the boat, and he stood on the floor of the sea. The serpent, hissing and lashing with pain, was drawn up through the vast depths of mid-ocean. The sea, away to the horizon, was covered with poisonous foam. High waves rose like tossing mountains over the vast expanse. Heavy clouds met the waters, and Thor's lightnings darted amid the seething billows. The horrid coils of the great serpent rose above the sea, glistening with venom, and his huge jaws gaped as he strove to seize his powerful enemy.

Thor grasped him in his arms, and the struggle grew fiercer still. Sheets of poisonous foam mixed with the clouds. The crashing of the thunder mingled with the loud hissing of the serpent; and except for the lightning, darkness covered the sea. Thor loosed his hold of the monster for an instant that he might hurl Mjöllnir at his head. Then the giant, who saw with fear and hatred the triumph of the god, cut the line; and with a long hiss of vengeful hate, the serpent sank back into the sea; there to await Ragnarök, the Twilight of the Gods.

Thor's rage and disappointment knew no bounds. He struck the giant a blow that sent him reeling from his boat into the boiling sea. Then he himself started on foot through the ocean, carrying the boat and all it contained. But Hymir recovered, and reached the shore soon after Thor.

They supped upon the two whales that the giant had caught. As soon as they had finished eating, Thor asked for the famous kettle, Mile-deep, hinting that Hymir might fear the consequences should he refuse to give it to him.

'Asa-Thor,' said the giant, 'you are asking a great favour, and you should give me one more proof of your strength before expecting me to do so much for you.' Rising from his seat, he took from a shelf a huge drinking-cup and, handing it to Thor, said, 'If you can break this cup, you shall have the kettle!'

Thor first threw the cup at an upright stone that served as a seat. The stone broke in two, but the cup remained whole. Then, with all his might, he flung it at one of the pillars of the hall. The column was shattered, but the cup was unhurt, showing not even a dent.

Then Tyr's mother whispered in Thor's ear, 'Strike at the head of Hymir; that is harder than any cup.'

Tightening his belt of strength, Thor again threw the cup, and this time full at Hymir's forehead. The cup was shattered to atoms.

Then was Hymir astounded and troubled. 'That was a good cup,' he said. 'Never again can I say, when the beer is handed to me, "Beer, thou art too hot."' And thinking it best to be rid of so dangerous a guest as soon as possible, he said to Thor, 'Now 'tis to be seen whether you can carry Mile-deep out of our dwelling.'

Tyr went up to the huge iron pot, and tried to lift it; but he could only tip it a little toward one side. Then Thor, with his iron gloves, grasped it by the brim, while his feet burst through the floor; and putting it upon his head, he started off, the rings jingling about his heels. Tyr followed him.

They had not gone far when they heard a loud noise behind them; and turning around they saw a mighty band of frost giants, with Hymir at their head. Some brandished great stone clubs, while others carried boulders and blocks of ice to throw at the Æsir; they shouted and roared as they came on. Then Thor put down Mile-deep, and grasping Mjöllnir, hurled it at the savage crew. Instantly all was still; and in place of the noisy giants, a line of snowy mountains raised their heads to the sky.

Thor and Tyr soon reached the place where the goats were tied, and putting the kettle into the chariot, drove rapidly toward Ægir's halls. They were delayed a little because the goat whose thigh-bone had been injured fell down, and then went lame. But in spite of this, they were not long in reaching Ægir's palace. The sea-god welcomed them, but looked with dismay at Mile-deep, knowing how great a brewing there would have to be in the future, when he feasted the gods.

IN THE GIANT'S HOUSE

as told by Abbie Farewell Brown

Although Thor had slain Thiassi the giant builder, Thrym the thief, Hrungnir and Hymir, and had rid the world of whole families of wicked giants, there remained many others in Jötunheim to do their evil deeds and to plot mischief against both gods and men; and of these Geirröd was the fiercest and the wickedest. He and his two ugly daughters – Gialp of the red eyes, and Greip of the black teeth – lived in a large palace among the mountains, where Geirröd had his treasures of iron and copper, silver and gold; for, since the death of Thrym, Geirröd was the Lord of the Mines, and all the riches that came out of the earth-caverns belonged to him.

Thrym had been Geirröd's friend, and the tale of Thrym's death through the might of Thor and his hammer had made Geirröd very sad and angry. 'If I could but catch Thor, now, without his weapons,' he said to his daughters, 'what a lesson I would give him! How I would punish him for his deeds against us giants!'

'Oh, what would you do, father?' cried Gialp, twinkling her cruel red eyes, and working her claw fingers as if she would like to fasten them in Thor's golden beard.

'Oh, what would you do, father?' cried Greip, smacking her lips and grinding her black teeth as if she would like a bite out of Thor's stout arm.

'Do to him!' growled Geirröd fiercely. 'Do to him! Gr-r-r! I would chew him all up! I would break his bones into little bits! I would smash him into jelly!'

'Oh, good, good! Do it, father, and then give him to us to play with,' cried Gialp and Greip, dancing up and down till the hills trembled and all the frightened sheep ran home to their folds thinking that there must be an earthquake; for Gialp was as tall as a pine tree and many times as thick, while Greip, her little sister, was as large around as a haystack and high as a flagstaff. They both hoped some day to be as huge as their father, whose legs were so long that he could step across the river valleys from one hilltop to another, just as we human folk cross a brook on stepping-stones; and his arms were so stout that he could lift a yoke of oxen in each fist, as if they were red-painted toys.

Geirröd shook his head at his two playful daughters and sighed. 'We must catch Master Thor first, my girls, before we do these fine things to him. We must catch him without his mighty hammer that never fails him, and without his belt that doubles his strength whenever he puts it on, or even I cannot chew and break and smash him as he deserves; for with these his weapons he is the mightiest creature in the whole world, and I would rather meddle with thunder and lightning than with him. Let us wait, children.'

Then Gialp and Greip pouted and sulked like two great babies who cannot have the new plaything which they want; and very ugly they were to see, with tears as big as oranges rolling down their cheeks.

Sooner than they expected they came very near to having their heart's desire fulfilled. And if it had happened as they wished, and if Asgard had lost its goodliest hero, its strongest defence, that would have been red Loki's fault, all Loki's evil planning; for you are now to hear of the wickedest thing that up to this time Loki had ever done. As you know, it was Loki who was Thor's bitterest enemy; and for many months he had been awaiting the chance to repay the Thunder Lord for the dole which Thor had brought upon him at the time of the dwarf's gifts to Asgard.

This is how it came about: Loki had long remembered the fun of skimming as a great bird in Freyja's falcon feathers. He had longed to borrow the wings once again and to fly away over the round world to see what he could see; for he thought that so he could learn many secrets which he was not meant to know, and plan wonderful mischief without being found out. But Freyja would not again loan her feather dress to Loki. She owed him a grudge for naming her as Thrym's bride; and besides, she remembered his treatment of Idunn, and she did not trust his oily tongue and fine promises. So Loki saw no way but to borrow the feathers without leave; and this he did one day when Freyja was gone to ride in her chariot drawn by white cats. Loki put on the feather dress, as he had done twice before – once when he went to Jötunheim to bring back stolen Idunn and her magic apples, once when he went to find out about Thor's hammer.

Away he flew from Asgard as birdlike as you please, chuckling to himself with wicked thoughts. It did not make any particular difference to him where he went. It was such fun to flap and fly, skim and wheel, looking and feeling for all the world like a big brown falcon. He swooped low, thinking, 'I wonder what Freyja would say to see me now! Whee-e-e! How angry she would be!' Just then he spied the high wall of a palace on the mountains.

'Oho!' said Loki. 'I never saw that place before. It may be a giant's dwelling. I think this must be Jötunheim, from the bigness of things. I must just peep to see.' Loki was the most inquisitive of creatures, as wily-minded folk are apt to be.

Loki the falcon alighted and hopped to the wall, then giving a flap of his wings he flew up and up to the window ledge, where he perched and peered into the hall. And there within he saw the giant Geirröd with his daughters eating their dinner. They looked so ugly and so greedy, as they sat there gobbling their food in giant mouthfuls, that Loki on the window-sill could not help snickering to himself. Now at that sound Geirröd looked up and saw the big brown bird peeping in at the window.

'Heigha!' cried the giant to one of his servants. 'Go you and fetch me the big brown bird up yonder in the window.'

Then the servant ran to the wall and tried to climb up to get at Loki; but the window was so high that he could not reach. He jumped and slipped, scrambled and slipped, again and again, while Loki sat just above his clutching fingers, and chuckled so that he nearly fell from his perch. 'Te-he! Te-he!' chattered Loki in the falcon tongue. It was such fun to see the fellow grow black in the face with trying to reach him that Loki thought he would wait until the giant's fingers almost touched him, before flying away.

But Loki waited too long. At last, with a quick spring, the giant gained a hold upon the window ledge, and Loki was within reach. When Loki flapped his wings to fly, he found that his feet were tangled in the vine that grew upon the wall. He struggled and twisted with all his might – but in vain. There he was, caught fast. Then the servant grasped him by the legs, and so brought him to Geirröd, where he sat at table. Now Loki in his feather dress looked exactly like a falcon – except for his eyes. There was no hiding the wise and crafty look of Loki's eyes. As soon as Geirröd looked at him, he suspected that this was no ordinary bird.

'You are no falcon, you!' he cried. 'You are spying about my palace in disguise. Speak, and tell me who you are.' Loki was afraid to tell, because he knew the giants were angry with him for his part in Thrym's death – small though his part had really been in that great deed. So he kept his beak closed tight, and refused to speak. The giant stormed and raged and threatened to kill him; but still Loki was silent.

Then Geirröd locked the falcon up in a chest for three long months without food or water, to see how that would suit his bird-ship. You can imagine how hungry and thirsty Loki was at the end of that time – ready to tell anything he knew, and more also, for the sake of a crumb of bread and a drop of water.

So then Geirröd called through the keyhole, 'Well, Sir Falcon, now will you tell me who you are?' And this time Loki piped feebly, 'I am Loki of Asgard; give me something to eat!'

'Oho!' quoth the giant fiercely. 'You are that Loki who went with Thor to kill my brother Thrym! Oho! Well, you shall die for that, my feathered friend!'

'No, no!' screamed Loki. 'Thor is no friend of mine. I love the giants far better! One of them is my wife!' – which was indeed true, as were few of Loki's words.

'Then if Thor is no friend of yours, to save your life will you bring him into my power?' asked Geirröd.

Loki's eyes gleamed wickedly among the feathers. Here all at once was his chance to be free, and to have his revenge upon Thor, his worst enemy. 'Ay, that I will!' he cried eagerly. 'I will bring Thor into your power.'

So Geirröd made him give a solemn promise to do that wrong; and upon this he loosed Loki from the chest and gave him food. Then they formed the wicked plan together, while Gialp and Greip, the giant's ugly daughters, listened and smacked their lips.

Loki was to persuade Thor to come with him to Geirrödsgard. More: he must come without his mighty hammer, and without the iron gloves of power, and without the belt of strength; for so only could the giant have Thor at his mercy.

After their wicked plans were made, Loki bade a friendly farewell to Geirröd and his daughters and flew back to Asgard as quickly as he could. You may be sure he had a sound scolding from Freyja for stealing her feather dress and for keeping it so long. But he told such a pitiful story of being kept prisoner by a cruel giant, and he looked in truth so pale and thin from his long fast, that the gods were fain to pity him and to believe his story, in spite of the many times that he had deceived them. Indeed, most of his tale was true, but he told only half of the truth; for he spoke no word of his promise to the giant. This he kept hidden in his breast.

Now, one day not long after this, Loki invited Thor to go on a journey with him to visit a new friend who, he said, was anxious to know the Thunder Lord. Loki was so pleasant in his manner and seemed so frank in his speech that Thor, whose heart was simple and unsuspicious, never dreamed of any wrong, not even when Loki added, 'And by the by, my Thor, you must leave behind your hammer, your belt and your gloves; for it would show little courtesy to wear such weapons in the home of a new friend.'

Thor carelessly agreed; for he was pleased with the idea of a new adventure, and with the thought of making a new friend. Besides, on their last journey together, Loki had behaved so well that Thor believed him to have changed his evil ways and to have become his friend. So together they set off in Thor's goat chariot, without weapons of any kind except those which Loki secretly carried. Loki chuckled as they rattled over the clouds, and if Thor had seen the look in his eyes, he would have turned the chariot back to Asgard and to safety, where he had left gentle Sif his wife. But Thor did not notice, and so they rumbled on.

Soon they came to the gate of Giant Land. Thor thought this strange, for he knew they were like to find few friends of his dwelling among the Big Folk. For the first time he began to suspect Loki of some treacherous scheme. However, he said nothing, and pretended to be as gay and careless as before. But he thought of a plan to find out the truth.

Close by the entrance was the cave of Grid, a good giantess, who alone of all her race was a friend of Thor and of the folk in Asgard.

'I will alight here for a moment, Loki,' said Thor carelessly. 'I long for a draught of water. Hold you the goats tightly by the reins until I return.'

So he went into the cave and got his draught of water. But while he was drinking, he questioned good mother Grid to some purpose.

'Who is this friend Geirröd whom I go to see?' he asked her.

'Geirröd your friend! You go to see Geirröd!' she exclaimed. 'He is the wickedest giant of us all, and no friend to you. Why do you go, dear Thor?'

'H'm!' muttered Thor. 'Red Loki's mischief again!' He told her of the visit that Loki had proposed, and how he had left at home the belt, the gloves and the hammer which made him stronger than any giant. Then Grid was frightened.

'Go not, go not, Thor!' she begged. 'Geirröd will kill you, and those ugly girls, Gialp and Greip, will have the pleasure of crunching your bones. Oh, I know them well, the hussies!'

But Thor declared that he would go, whether or no. 'I have promised Loki that I will go,' he said, 'and go I will; for I always keep my word.'

'Then you shall have three little gifts of me,' quoth she. 'Here is my belt of power – for I also have one like your own.' And she buckled about his waist a great belt, at whose touch he felt his strength redoubled. 'This is my iron glove,' she said, as she put one on his mighty hand, 'and with it, as with your own, you can handle lightning and touch unharmed the hottest of red-hot metal. And here, last of all,' she added, 'is Gridarvöll, my good staff, which you may find useful. Take them, all three; and may Sif see you safe at home again by their aid.'

Thor thanked her and went out once more to join Loki, who never suspected what had happened in the cave. For the belt and the glove were hidden under Thor's cloak. And as for the staff, it was quite ordinary looking, as if Thor might have picked it up anywhere along the road.

On they journeyed until they came to the river Vimer, the greatest of all rivers, which roared and tossed in a terrible way between them and the shore which they wanted to reach. It seemed impossible to cross. But Thor drew his belt a little tighter, and planting Grid's staff firmly on the bottom, stepped out into the stream. Loki clung behind to his cloak, frightened out of his wits. But Thor waded on bravely, his strength doubled by Grid's belt, and his steps supported by her magic staff. Higher and higher the waves washed over his knees, his waist, his shoulders, as if they were fierce to drown him. And Thor said:

'Ho there, river Vimer! Do not grow any larger, I pray. It is of no use. The more you crowd upon me, the mightier I grow with my belt and my staff!'

But lo! As he nearly reached the other side, Thor spied someone hiding close down by the bank of the river. It was Gialp of the red eyes, the big elder daughter of Geirröd. She was splashing the water upon Thor, making the great waves that rolled up and threatened to drown him.

'Oho!' cried he. 'So it is you who are making the river rise, big little girl. We must see to that.' And seizing a huge boulder, he hurled it at her. It hit her with a thud, for Thor's aim never missed. Giving a scream as loud as a steam-whistle, Gialp limped home as best she could to tell her father, and to prepare a warm reception for the stranger who bore Loki at his back.

When Thor had pulled himself out of the river by some bushes, he soon came to the palace which Loki had first sighted in his falcon dress. And there he found everything most courteously made ready for him. He and Loki were received like dear old friends, with shouts of rejoicing and ringing of bells. Geirröd himself came out to meet them, and would have embraced his new friend Thor; but the Thunder Lord merely seized him by the hand and gave him so hearty a squeeze with the iron glove that the giant howled with pain. Yet he could say nothing, for Thor looked pleased and gentle. And Geirröd said to himself, 'Ho, ho, my fine little Thor! I will soon pay you for that handshake, and for many things beside.'

All this time Gialp and Greip did not appear, and Loki also had taken himself away, to be out of danger when the hour of Thor's death should come. For he feared that dreadful things might happen before Thor died; and he did not want to be remembered by the big fist of the companion whom he had betrayed. Loki, having kept his promise to the giant, was even now far on the road back to Asgard, where he meant with a sad face to tell the gods that Thor had been slain by a horrible giant; but never to tell them how.

So Thor was all alone when the servants led him to the chamber which Geirröd had made ready for his dear friend. It was a wonderfully fine chamber, to be sure; but the strange thing about it was that among the furnishings there was but one chair, a giant chair, with a drapery all about the legs. Now Thor was very weary with his long journey, and he sat down in the chair to rest. Then – wonderful to tell! – if elevators had been invented in those days, he might have thought he was in one. For instantly the seat of the chair shot up towards the roof, and against this he was in danger of being crushed as Geirröd had longed to see him. But quick as a flash Thor raised the staff which good old Grid had given him, and pushed it against the rafters with all his might to stop his upward journey. It was a tremendous push that he gave. Something cracked; something crashed; the chair fell to the ground as Thor leaped off the seat, and there were two terrible screams.

Then Thor found – what do you think? Why, that Gialp and Greip, the giant's daughters, had hidden under the seat of the chair, and had lifted it up on their backs to crush Thor against the roof! But instead of that, it was Thor who had broken their backs, so that they lay dead upon the floor like limp rag dolls.

Now this little exercise had only given Thor an excellent appetite for supper. So that when word came bidding him to the banquet, he was very glad.

'First', said big Geirröd, grinning horribly, for he did not know what had happened to his daughters, 'first we will see some games, friend Thor.'

Then Thor came into the hall, where fires were burning in great chimney places along the walls. 'It is here that we play our little games,' cried Geirröd. And on the moment, seizing a pair of tongs, he snatched a red-hot wedge of iron from one of the fires and hurled it straight at Thor's head. But Thor was quicker than he. Swift as a flash he caught the flying spark in his iron glove, and calling forth all the might of Grid's belt, he cast the wedge back at the giant. Geirröd dodged behind an iron pillar, but it was in vain. Thor's might was such as no iron could meet. Like a bolt of lightning the wedge passed through the pillar, through Geirröd himself, through the thick wall of the palace, and buried itself deep in the ground, where it lodges to this day, unless someone has dug it up to sell for old iron.

So perished Geirröd and his children, one of the wickedest families of giants that ever lived in Jötunheim. And so Thor escaped from the snares of Loki, who had never done a deed worse than this.

When Thor returned home to Asgard, where from Loki's lying tale he found all the gods mourning him as dead, you can fancy what a joyful reception he had. But for Loki, the false-hearted, false-tongued traitor to them all, there was only hatred. He no longer had any friends among the good folk. The wicked giants and the monsters of Utgard were now his only friends, for he had grown to be like them, and even these did not trust him overmuch.

THOR'S DUEL

as told by Abbie Farewell Brown

In the days that are past a wonderful race of horses pastured in the meadows of heaven, steeds more beautiful and more swift than any which the world knows today. There was Hrîmfaxi, the black, sleek horse who drew the chariot of Night across the sky and scattered the dew from his foaming bit. There was Glad, behind whose flying heels sped the swift chariot of Day. His mane was yellow with gold, and from it beamed light which made the whole world bright. Then there were the two shining horses of the sun, Arvakur the watchful and Alsvith the rapid; and the nine fierce battle-chargers of the nine Valkyries, who bore the bodies of fallen heroes from the field of fight to the blessedness of Valhalla. Each of the gods had his own glorious steed, with such pretty names as Gold-mane and Silver-top, Light-foot and Precious-stone; these galloped with their masters over clouds and through the blue air, blowing flame from their nostrils and glinting sparks from their fiery eyes. The Æsir would have been poor indeed without their faithful mounts, and few would be the stories to tell in which these noble creatures do not bear at least a part.

But best of all the horses of heaven was Sleipnir, the eight-legged steed of Father Odin, who because he was so well supplied with sturdy feet could gallop faster over land and sea than any horse which ever lived. Sleipnir was snow-white and beautiful to see, and Odin was very fond and proud of him, you may be sure. He loved to ride forth upon his good horse's back to meet whatever adventure might be upon the way, and sometimes they had wild times together.

One day Odin galloped off from Asgard upon Sleipnir straight towards Jötunheim and the Land of Giants, for it was long since All-Father had been to the cold country, and he wished to see how its mountains and ice-rivers looked. Now as he galloped along a wild road, he met a huge giant standing beside his giant steed.

'Who goes there?' cried the giant gruffly, blocking the way so that Odin could not pass. 'You with the golden helmet, who are you, who ride so famously through air and water? For I have been watching you from this mountain-top. Truly, that is a fine horse which you bestride.'

'There is no finer horse in all the world,' boasted Odin. 'Have you not heard of Sleipnir, the pride of Asgard? I will match him against any of your big, clumsy giant horses.'

'Ho!' roared the giant angrily. 'An excellent horse he is, your little Sleipnir. But I warrant he is no match for my Gullfaxi here. Come, let us try a race; and at its end I shall pay you for your insult to our horses of Jötunheim.'

So saying, the giant, whose ugly name was Hrungnir, sprang upon his horse and spurred straight at Odin in the narrow way. Odin turned and galloped back towards Asgard with all his might; for not only must he prove his horse's speed, but he must save himself and Sleipnir from the anger of the giant, who was one of the fiercest and wickedest of all his fierce and wicked race.

How the eight slender legs of Sleipnir twinkled through the blue sky! How his nostrils quivered and shot forth fire and smoke! Like a flash of lightning he darted across the sky, and the giant horse rumbled and thumped along close behind like the thunder following the flash.

'Hi, hi!' yelled the giant. 'After them, Gullfaxi! And when we have overtaken the two, we will crush their bones between us!'

'Speed, speed, my Sleipnir!' shouted Odin. 'Speed, good horse, or you will never again feed in the dewy pastures of Asgard with the other horses. Speed, speed, and bring us safe within the gates!'

Well Sleipnir understood what his master said, and well he knew the way. Already the rainbow bridge was in sight, with Heimdal the watchman prepared to let them in. His sharp eyes had spied them afar, and had recognized the flash of Sleipnir's white body and of Odin's golden helmet. Gallop and thud! The twelve hoofs were upon the bridge, the giant horse close behind the other. At last Hrungnir knew where he was, and into what danger he was rushing. He pulled at the reins and tried to stop his great beast. But Gullfaxi was tearing along at too terrible a speed. He could not stop. Heimdal threw open the gates of Asgard, and in galloped Sleipnir with his precious burden, safe. Close upon them bolted in Gullfaxi, bearing his giant master, puffing and purple in the face from hard riding and anger. Cling-clang! Heimdal had shut and barred the gates, and there was the giant prisoned in the castle of his enemies.

Now the Æsir were courteous folk, unlike the giants, and they were not anxious to take advantage of a single enemy thus thrown into their power. They invited him to enter Valhalla with them, to rest and sup before the long journey of his return. Thor was not present, so they filled for the giant the great cups which Thor was wont to drain, for they were nearest to the giant size. But you remember that Thor was famous for his power to drink deep. Hrungnir's head was not so steady: Thor's draught was too much for him. He soon lost his wits, of which he had but few; and a witless giant is a most dreadful creature. He raged like a madman, and threatened to pick up Valhalla like a toy house and carry it home with him to Jötunheim. He said he would pull Asgard to pieces and slay all the gods except Freyja the fair and Sif, the golden-haired wife of Thor, whom he would carry off like little dolls for his toy house.

The Æsir knew not what to do, for Thor and his hammer were not there to protect them, and Asgard seemed in danger with this enemy within its very walls. Hrungnir called for more and more mead, which Freyja alone dared to bring and set before him. And the more he drank the fiercer he became. At last the Æsir could bear no longer his insults and his violence. Besides, they feared that there would be no more mead left for their banquets if this unwelcome visitor should keep Freyja pouring out for him Thor's mighty goblets. They bade Heimdal blow his horn and summon Thor; and this Heimdal did in a trice.

Now rumbling and thundering in his chariot of goats came Thor. He dashed into the hall, hammer in hand, and stared in amazement at the unwieldy guest whom he found there. 'A giant feasting in Asgard hall!' he roared. 'This is a sight which I never saw before. Who gave the insolent fellow leave to sit in my place? And why does fair Freyja wait upon him as if he were some noble guest at a feast of the high gods? I will slay him at once!' And he raised the hammer to keep his word.

Thor's coming had sobered the giant somewhat, for he knew that this was no enemy to be trifled with. He looked at Thor sulkily and said: 'I am Odin's guest. He invited me to this banquet, and therefore I am under his protection.'

'You shall be sorry that you accepted the invitation,' cried Thor, balancing his hammer and looking very fierce; for Sif had sobbed in his ear how the giant had threatened to carry her away.

Hrungnir now rose to his feet and faced Thor boldly, for the sound of Thor's gruff voice had restored his scattered wits. 'I am here alone and without weapons,' he said. 'You would do ill to slay me now. It would be little like the noble Thor, of whom we hear tales, to do such a thing. The world will count you braver if you let me go and meet me later in single combat, when we shall both be fairly armed.'

Thor dropped the hammer to his side. 'Your words are true,' he said, for he was a just and honourable fellow.

'I was foolish to leave my shield and stone club at home,' went on the giant. 'If I had my arms with me, we would fight at this moment. But I name you a coward if you slay me now, an unarmed enemy.'

'Your words are just,' quoth Thor again. 'I have never before been challenged by any foe. I will meet you, Hrungnir, at your Stone City, midway between heaven and earth. And there we will fight a duel to see which of us is the better fellow.'

Hrungnir departed for Stone City in Jötunheim; and great was the excitement of the other giants when they heard of the duel which one of their number was to fight with Thor, the deadliest enemy of their race.

'We must be sure that Hrungnir wins the victory!' they cried. 'It will never do to have Asgard victorious in the first duel that we have fought with her champion. We will make a second hero to aid Hrungnir.'

All the giants set to work with a will. They brought great buckets of moist clay, and heaping them up into a huge mound, moulded the mass with their giant hands as a sculptor does his image, until they had made a man of clay, an immense dummy, nine miles high and three miles wide. 'Now we must make him live; we must put a heart into him!' they cried. But they could find no heart big enough until they thought of taking that of a mare, and that fitted nicely. A mare's heart is the most cowardly one that beats.

Hrungnir's heart was a three-cornered piece of hard stone. His head also was of stone, and likewise the great shield which he held before him when he stood outside Stone City waiting for Thor to come to the duel. Over his shoulder he carried his club, and that also was of stone, the kind from which whetstones are made, hard and terrible. By his side stood the huge clay man, Möckuralfi, and they were a dreadful sight to see, these two vast bodies whom Thor must encounter.

But at the very first sight of Thor, who came thundering to the place with swift Thialfi his servant, the timid mare's heart in the man of clay throbbed with fear; he trembled so that his knees knocked together, and his nine miles of height rocked unsteadily. Thialfi ran up to Hrungnir and began to mock him, saying, 'You are careless, giant. I fear you do not know what a mighty enemy has come to fight you. You hold your shield in front of you; but that will serve you nothing. Thor has seen this. He has only to go down into the earth and he can attack you conveniently from beneath your very feet.'

At this terrifying news Hrungnir hastened to throw his shield upon the ground and to stand upon it, so that he might be safe from Thor's under-stroke. He grasped his heavy club with both hands and waited. He had not long to wait. There came a blinding flash of lightning and a peal of crashing thunder. Thor had cast his hammer into space. Hrungnir raised his club with both hands and hurled it against the hammer which he saw flying towards him. The two mighty weapons met in the air with an earsplitting shock. Hard as was the stone of the giant's club, it was like glass against the power of Mjöllnir. The club was dashed into pieces; some fragments fell upon the earth; and these, they say, are the rocks from which whetstones are made unto this day. They are so hard that men use them to sharpen knives and axes and scythes. One splinter of the hard stone struck Thor himself in the forehead, with so fierce a blow that he fell forward upon the ground, and Thialfi feared that he was killed. But Mjöllnir, not even stopped in its course by meeting the giant's club, sped straight to Hrungnir and crushed his stony skull, so that he fell forward over Thor, and his foot lay on the fallen hero's neck. And that was the end of the giant whose head and heart were of stone.

Meanwhile Thialfi the swift had fought with the man of clay, and had found little trouble in toppling him to earth. For the mare's cowardly heart in his great body gave him little strength to meet Thor's faithful servant; and the trembling limbs of Möckuralfi soon yielded to Thialfi's hearty blows. He fell like an unsteady tower of blocks, and his brittle bulk shivered into a thousand fragments.

Thialfi ran to his master and tried to raise him. The giant's great foot still rested upon his neck, and all Thialfi's strength could not move it away. Swift as the wind he ran for the other Æsir, and when they heard that great Thor, their champion, had fallen and seemed like one dead, they came rushing to the spot in horror and confusion. Together they all attempted to raise Hrungnir's foot from Thor's neck that they might see whether their hero lived or no. But all their efforts were in vain. The foot was not to be lifted by Æsir-might.

At this moment a second hero appeared upon the scene. It was Magni, the son of Thor himself; Magni, who was but three days old, yet already in his babyhood he was almost as big as a giant and had nearly the strength of his father. This wonderful youngster came running to the place where his father lay surrounded by a group of sad-faced and despairing gods. When Magni saw what the matter was, he seized Hrungnir's enormous foot in both his hands, heaved his broad young shoulders, and in a moment Thor's neck was free of the weight which was crushing it.

Best of all, it proved that Thor was not dead, only stunned by the blow of the giant's club and by his fall. He stirred, sat up painfully, and looked around him at the group of eager friends. 'Who lifted the weight from my neck?' he asked.

'It was I, father,' answered Magni modestly. Thor clasped him in his arms and hugged him tight, beaming with pride and gratitude.

'Truly, you are a fine child!' he cried. 'One to make glad your father's heart. Now as a reward for your first great deed you shall have a gift from me. The swift horse of Hrungnir shall be yours – that same Gullfaxi who was the beginning of all this trouble. You shall ride Gullfaxi; only a giant steed is strong enough to bear the weight of such an infant prodigy as you, my Magni.'

Now this word did not wholly please Father Odin, for he thought that a horse so excellent ought to belong to him. He took Thor aside and argued that but for him there would have been no duel, no horse to win. Thor answered simply:

'True, Father Odin, you began this trouble. But I have fought your battle, destroyed your enemy, and suffered great pain for you. Surely, I have won the horse fairly and may give it to whom I choose. My son, who has saved me, deserves a horse as good as any. Yet, as you have proved, even Gullfaxi is scarce a match for your Sleipnir. Verily, Father Odin, you should be content with the best.' Odin said no more.

Now Thor went home to his cloud-palace in Thrudvang. And there he was healed of all his hurts except that which the splinter of stone had made in his forehead. For the stone was embedded so fast that it could not be taken out, and Thor suffered sorely therefor. Sif, his yellow-haired wife, was in despair, knowing not what to do. At last she bethought her of the wise woman, Groa, who had skill in all manner of herbs and witch charms. Sif sent for Groa, who lived all alone and sad because her husband Örvandil had disappeared, she knew not whither. Groa came to Thor and, standing beside his bed while he slept, sang strange songs and gently waved her hands over him. Immediately the stone in his forehead began to loosen, and Thor opened his eyes.

'The stone is loosening, the stone is coming out!' he cried. 'How can I reward you, gentle dame? Prithee, what is your name?'

'My name is Groa,' answered the woman, weeping, 'wife of Örvandil who is lost.'

'Now, then, I can reward you, kind Groa!' cried Thor. 'For I can bring you tidings of your husband. I met him in the cold country, in Jötunheim, the Land of Giants, which you know I sometimes visit for a bit of good hunting. It was by Elivâgar's icy river that I met Örvandil, and there was no way for him to cross. So I put him in an iron basket and myself bore him over the flood. Br-r-r! But that is a cold land! His feet stuck out through the meshes of the basket, and when we reached the other side one of his toes was frozen stiff. So I broke it off and tossed it up into the sky that it might become a star. To prove that what I relate is true, Groa, there is the new star shining over us at this very moment. Look! From this day it shall be known to men as Örvandil's Toe. Do not you weep any longer. After all, the loss of a toe is a little thing; and I promise that your husband shall soon return to you, safe and sound, but for that small token of his wanderings in the land where visitors are not welcome.'

At these joyful tidings poor Groa was so overcome that she fainted. And that put an end to the charm which she was weaving to loosen the stone from Thor's forehead. The stone was not yet wholly free, and thenceforth it was in vain to attempt its removal; Thor must always wear the splinter in his forehead. Groa could never forgive herself for the carelessness which had thus made her skill vain to help one to whom she had reason to be so grateful.

Now because of the bit of whetstone in Thor's forehead, folk of olden times were very careful how they used a whetstone; and especially they knew that they must not throw or drop one on the floor. For when they did so, the splinter in Thor's forehead was jarred, and the good Asa suffered great pain.

THE BINDING OF THE WOLF

as told by Mary Litchfield

Odin returned to Asgard after a long absence, and all noticed that he looked more grave and majestic than ever. He spoke to no one but Frigg,[21] his wife, of the wonderful things he had seen and heard. Frigg never revealed what was told her in confidence.

Loki was away when Odin returned; and the latter at once took steps to place the children of the treacherous god and the witch of the iron-wood where they could do no harm.

The children were worthy of their parents. One was a wolf, Fenrir, not yet fully grown; him Odin had brought to Asgard and given in charge of Tyr,[22] one of the strongest and bravest of the Æsir. Another was a dangerous serpent; and he was put into the river, Ocean, that surrounded Midgard, the world of men. As soon as he touched the bottom of the sea he began to grow, and grew so fast that before long he reached entirely around Midgard; and his tail, finding no other place, grew down his throat. He was called the Midgard serpent from that time forth. But more dreadful in appearance than either of these monsters was the third. She had the form of a woman, but the hard heart of her mother, the witch

---

21. Frigg is the usual form, but Frigga is sometimes preferred.

22. Son of Odin – one-armed god of war.

of the iron-wood; and half her body was of a deathly white colour, so that no one could bear to look upon her. Odin sent her to Urd, guardian of the fountain under the third root of the World Tree, and ruler of all the realms of the dead. She made this dreadful being queen of the world of torture under Niflheim.

Loki's last two children were well disposed of, for the present, at least; but the wolf, Fenrir, kept growing stronger and fiercer each day; and Tyr, powerful as he was, found it no easy matter to control him. After consulting together, the gods decided to bind him with an iron chain.

There was a smithy in Asgard, with the best facilities for making all kinds of metal things, such as chains, swords, shields and axes. And in this smithy the gods forged a chain larger and stronger than any that had ever been seen in Asgard. They took it to Fenrir and asked him to amuse them by showing his strength.

Fenrir was very proud of his strength; and as soon as he saw the chain, he knew he could easily break it.

So he let them bind him, standing quietly as they did so. When they had finished, he stretched his limbs, and the chain instantly broke in several places. The gods pretended to consider it a good joke, and praised the wolf for his strength, saying they would try the game again some day.

They now realized that to make a chain strong enough to bind the wolf was likely to prove no easy task. This time the most skilful workers in metal were secured, and they did their best to make the second chain the strongest that could possibly be forged. When it was finished, all declared that nothing like it had ever been seen in all the nine worlds.

They went to Fenrir as before; but when he saw them bringing a chain so heavy that it took several gods merely to drag it along the ground, his suspicions were aroused. He refused to be bound. Then they appealed to his pride till his strength swelled within him; and, eager to show his power, he let them wind the chain around till his whole body was covered with iron links. Then he rolled on the ground, and stretched his huge limbs, and the bonds burst as though made of some brittle metal. The gods dissembled their feelings as best they could, and praised the strength and courage of the wolf more than ever.

Odin, with his great wisdom, realized how important it was that Fenrir should be bound. Finding that Asgard could not produce a chain strong enough for that purpose, he sent Skirnir to the home of the dark elves to get one. For great as were the gods, the elves and giants knew more about some things than they did.

And indeed, the dark elves must have been very wise and skilful to have made the chain which they gave Skirnir. How they managed to get the materials of which it was composed is a mystery; for it was made of six things seldom seen in Asgard or Midgard, – namely: the footfalls of a cat, the beard of a woman, the roots of a mountain, the sinews of a bear, the breath of a fish and the spittle of birds. One could believe almost anything of a chain made of such things. It is no wonder that it was as soft and smooth as a silken string, and that its strength was greater than that of any chain made since the nine worlds were formed.

Skirnir did his errand very quickly, considering the long distance he had to go; and happy were the gods when he returned with the delicate, silken string. They felt sure of success now; for things made by the dark elves always possessed wonderful properties.

In order to disarm the suspicions of Fenrir, the gods planned an excursion to a rocky island, pretending that the sole object of the trip was amusement. The amusement was to consist mainly in trials of strength. Fenrir went with them. Had he discovered any chain, he would have suspected foul play; but there was nothing of the kind to be seen.

As soon as they reached the island, the sports began. They ran races, leaped over barriers, shot with bows, wrestled and, in short, did all those things that test men's strength and skill. After the trials were ended and the victors had been crowned, they sat on the grass near Fenrir, talking and jesting.

One of the gods then drew from his bosom the magic chain, and handing it to his neighbour, said, 'They say this cord is stronger than it looks. See if you can break it.' The one to whom it was given tried in vain; and then with a jest he passed it to the god next him, and so it went the rounds.

When all had tried and failed, Skirnir said, as though struck by a sudden thought, 'Let Fenrir try. He has strength in breaking chains, if he can do nothing else.'

So one of the gods held up the cord, saying, 'Would you like to try your strength on this little string, Fenrir? Perhaps you will scorn to be bound by so slight a thing; but it is too strong for our hands to break.'

The wolf refused the trial, for he suspected treachery. Then they taunted him, saying that only a coward would refuse to be bound by such a cobweb. Their taunts stirred Fenrir's pride; and he finally agreed to let them bind the chain about him, if one of their number would put his right hand into his jaws while it was being done, as a pledge of their good faith.

Upon this the gods looked at one another in dismay. But after an instant's pause, Tyr, well knowing what the result would be, stepped up to the wolf, and thrust his right hand into his jaws, saying, with a laugh, 'You see it is only a joke, Fenrir!'

The wolf let them bind him; and when the magic cord was tightly around, the gods moved away, all but Tyr, for they knew the struggle would be terrible.

The monster now stretched his limbs; and finding that the more he struggled the tighter grew the string, he bit Tyr's hand off at the wrist and then rolled on the ground, rending the air with his howls of rage and despair. When he had worn himself out with his desperate struggles, the gods secured him and took him back to Asgard.

Odin had him carried to a dark cave, on a rocky island, in the regions of torture below Niflheim.[23] He was chained to a rock that was sunk far into the earth, and his jaws were kept open by a sword that was thrust into them so that the hilt stood in the lower jaw and the point in the roof of his mouth. From his jaws flowed a poisonous river. There he would remain chained until Ragnarök, the Twilight of the Gods, should come.

Brave Tyr, by his sacrifice, had saved Asgard from a dangerous foe.

---

23. Rydberg describes the regions of torture in his *Teutonic Mythology*.

THE DEATH OF BALDR

as told by Mary Litchfield

Loki proposed one day that they should have some sports on the plains of Ida; and he named among other things the game of shooting at Baldr.

Toward sundown the Æsir went out upon the broad, green plain, and Baldr stood up in the midst of them. He stood there like a beautiful victim surrounded by his foes; but his face was peaceful, and he smiled to see how they enjoyed the strange sport.

At last, all had shot except Hodur. When his turn came, he had no weapon. Some say he was blind, and that was why he could not shoot. Just then Loki came up, and said, 'Here is a little arrow I found the other day; perhaps this will do.' And he gave Hodur a small, well-made arrow. Hodur took the arrow, fitted it to the string, and in an instant it was whizzing through the air. The next moment Baldr had fallen, pierced to the heart by the fatal weapon of mistletoe.

The gods were so astounded that at first no one moved. Then Thor sprang forward and lifted Baldr gently from the ground – but he was dead. All eyes were now turned towards Hodur; for the Æsir did not suspect that Loki was the real author of the deed.

Still, no one sought to avenge Baldr's death; for the laws of the peace-stead, where they were, permitted no violence.

Wailing and lamenting, they took up the body and went slowly toward the palace of Gladsheim. The birds stopped singing, and the flowers drooped as the dead god passed by. When Odin saw them coming, and knew that Baldr was killed, he bowed his head, and said, 'My son is dead! The light is gone from Asgard!' Frigg clasped him in her arms and vainly begged him to come back. The sorrow of Nanna, Baldr's wife, was too deep for tears. She did not speak or cry; but the colour left her cheek, and her eye grew dim.

BALDR'S FUNERAL

as told by Mary Litchfield

Baldr's body was placed in the great hall of his palace of 'Broad-shining-splendour'. He lay there as though asleep. His broad brow was peaceful, and his expression radiant and beautiful. Tall youths stood about him, clad in white and holding torches of sweet-smelling wood. Reverently they stood with bowed heads, while many came from distant places to look once more upon the purest of the gods. At intervals the youths chanted solemn hymns in a low tone; and at the end of each hymn came in the refrain, 'Baldr the Beautiful is dead!'

News of his death soon reached the world of men, and great was the sorrow felt at his loss.

Men reverenced Odin for his wisdom and his might in battle; Baldr, they loved. Even the light-elves, always gay and merry, wept for Baldr; and the dwarfs, when they heard of his death, began to search for jewels to be burnt with him. The stony hearts of the giants were softened, and they came in troops to see him, bringing great trees, to be burned in the funeral pile.

Baldr's ship, *Ringhorn*, was the largest ship in the world, and on that was built the funeral pile. The huge trees brought by the giants were first laid on; then smaller trees; and finally branches of all sweet-smelling woods. Over the boughs were laid mantles, beautifully wrought. Baldr's horse, richly caparisoned, was next placed upon the pile. And last, all who wished to honour the dead god brought gifts to be burnt with him. Odin gave his ring made by Sindri; Thor, a finely tempered sword; many of the goddesses brought their necklaces and bracelets; the dwarfs gave precious jewels; and the light-elves, having no possessions, strewed the pile with flowers.

When all was ready, they went to Baldr's palace. The youths who had been watching there placed the body upon a golden litter, and bore it slowly towards the ship. Behind them walked Nanna, supported by her maidens. She was clothed in white, and her long hair floated over her shoulders. The others, however, displayed all their magnificence in honour of the dead god. Odin was there with his wolves and his ravens. Frigg wore her richest garments, although her heart was sad. Freyr rode the boar with the golden bristles, and Freyja was in her chariot drawn by cats. Thor had his famous goats. Many gods rode steeds of great beauty. And even Heimdall had left his post at the northern end of Bifröst, and came mounted on Goldtop, whose mane shone like the sun.

A strange procession it was; gods, giants, elves and dwarfs, all uniting to honour the purest of the Æsir. And strange were the hymns they sang, as they slowly traversed the long road from Baldr's palace to the sea. The deep tones of the giants blended for once with the shrill, piping voices of the light-elves, as ancient battle-hymns and songs of peace rose upon the still air.

When they reached the ship, all stood silent, while Baldr's body was lifted upon the funeral pile. As the youths stepped down, they saw that Nanna had fallen, and her maidens were trying in vain to bring her back to life. Her heart had broken when she saw Baldr leaving her to go alone upon his last voyage. So they placed her beside him whom she had loved better than life itself.

Thor raised high his mighty hammer and consecrated the pile, while sharp lightnings flashed, and thunder sounded through the clear sky. The white sails were spread, the youths lighted the pile with their torches, and the ship Ringhorn left forever the shores of Asgard, and sailed towards the setting sun. As it sailed away, the smoke rose to heaven, and soon the whole ship was in flames; until at last it sank behind the western horizon in a blaze of glory.

HERMOD'S JOURNEY IN SEARCH OF BALDR

as told by Mary Litchfield

After Baldr's death Frigg asked whether anyone would be willing to go to the lower world in search of him, while preparations for his funeral were going on in Asgard. Hermod, the messenger-god, offered to go, and started off at once, on Sleipnir, the swiftest of steeds.

The Æsir watched eagerly for his return, and loud shouts went up when he appeared. He entered the great hall of Gladsheim, where all were gathered, and approaching Odin, said: 'I bring you hope! Baldr greets you, and sends again this ring made by the dwarfs, which he asks you to keep always in remembrance of him.' Then turning to Frigg, he gave her a carpet and other gifts from Nanna; and to Fulla, one of her maidens, a finger-ring. After bestowing these gifts, and giving each one a message from Baldr, he said:

'I went, as you know, by the bridge Bifröst, whose northern end is near Niflheim. For nine nights Sleipnir bore me through valleys deep and dark, and at last I reached the river Gjöll, which is spanned by the Gjallar bridge, whose roof is of glittering gold. As Sleipnir stepped upon the bridge, the maid Modgud, who keeps it, asked me my name and my parentage, saying that the day before five bands of dead men had ridden over, and had not made as much noise as Sleipnir's hoofs made in just striking the bridge.

'And', she added, 'it did not shake beneath them as it does

beneath you.' Then she looked closely at me, and said: 'You have not the complexion of the dead; why do you ride here on your way to the realms of Urd?' I told her I came seeking Baldr, and I asked her whether he had passed that way. She said that he had ridden over the Gjallar bridge; and she then told me how to go, that I might find him.

'I went as she bade me, and came at last to that part of Mimir's realms where rules Delling, the elf of the dawn. After going far into a thick forest I found the castle she had described. It was as magnificent as Gladsheim; indeed, I cannot begin to tell of its beauty and grandeur; but it was surrounded by a wall so high that no intruder could hope to get near. Fortunately, I rode Sleipnir; no other steed would have served me then. With one bound he cleared the high wall, and I found myself in a lovely garden. Before me was the castle. The door was open, so I stepped in; and the first person I saw was Baldr. He sat upon a kind of throne. Nanna was beside him. The castle was filled with beings who were evidently rejoicing at Baldr's coming. They did not seem to be gods, and yet were fairer and nobler than mortals.

'Baldr rose to greet me as I entered, and his face beamed with the same expression of peace and good-will that it wore when he was among us. And Nanna looked as happy as on the day when she first came to Asgard as Baldr's wife. I was filled with wonder.

'Baldr said kindly: 'Hermod, you are astonished at seeing us so well and so happy here in the lower world. We have been warmly welcomed by the people who live in this beautiful castle, and their golden mead has the virtues of Idunn's apples, and even more; for it has restored Nanna and myself to the fullest enjoyment of life.'

'"Who are these people, Baldr?" I inquired.

"'I may not tell you all about them," Baldr replied; 'but they are my loyal subjects, and repay my love and care with the greatest devotion.'

'Then we talked of Asgard, and of you all, as we drank the golden mead. I asked Baldr whether he would return to us should the great goddess of the realms of death allow him to do so.

'He pondered deeply, and then replied, "Yes, I would return were it allowed; not wholly for my own pleasure – for I already love my new subjects; but because you all grieve so for my loss in the upper worlds.' And he added with a smile, 'We are very happy here."

'When I left the palace, he and Nanna put into my hands the gifts I have brought, and seemed loath to part with me.

'From there I went south, to the land of Urd, so well known to you all. I found the mighty goddess seated by her well, her two sisters near. When I begged her to allow Baldr to return to Asgard, she said, 'Is Baldr unhappy in the lower world?'

"'No," I replied; "but we grieve for him in Asgard. The sun itself seems to have lost its brightness since Baldr left us; and not the gods alone, all mankind, the dwarfs and the elves, and even the stony giants, long for Baldr's return."'

"'Are you sure that all mourn for Baldr?" said the dread goddess, in her deep, solemn voice.

"'Yes, all," I replied.

'Then after a pause, she said slowly, "Should every creature wish for his return, should each one weep for him, he might go back to Asgard; not otherwise. Remember, all must weep!"

'And so I bring you hope; for surely all will weep for Baldr; he was so loved by all.'

Messengers were sent far and wide to bid all beings weep for

Baldr; even the trees and stones. On swift steeds the heralds rushed along, crying, 'Baldr the Beautiful is dead! Weep for him!' Over high mountains, through deep valleys, by the lonely shore, everywhere they went, crying, 'Baldr the Beautiful is dead! Weep for him!' And as they heard the cry, all beings, even the rocks and the stones, wept for the god beloved of gods and men.

The messengers were going home, rejoicing in their success, when they met a giantess who called herself Thok. As she gazed at them with her cold, unfeeling eyes, they cried, 'Baldr the Beautiful is dead! Weep for him!' But she answered,

'Thok will weep
With dry tears
For Baldr's death;
Neither in life nor in death
Gave he me gladness.
Let Hel keep what she has.'

As she spoke these words, the giantess laughed a hard, mocking laugh, and disappeared; and the messengers went slowly back to Asgard. No one knew until afterwards that the giantess was really Loki in disguise.

LOKI AT ÆGIR'S FEAST

as told by Mary Litchfield

Ægir had a palace at the bottom of the ocean, in the western part of the lower world. It was an enormous building, and its many peaks and towers seemed to undulate as they rose through the dim waters. Near it were forests of sea-trees that lifted their palm-like branches as high as the castle's loftiest pinnacles. Beside the pearl walls glowed corals, red or rose-coloured, and over them ran vines of delicate green.

Ægir had asked all the gods to a feast. The huge kettle procured by Thor and Tyr was to be used for the first time; so there would doubtless be mead enough to go round.

As they entered the deep-sea palace, the gods beheld a scene of rare beauty. The large hall rose to a great height, its roof supported by pillars of coral. From the roof hung golden lamps, flooding the hall with light. Sea-plants grew in all the recesses, and from shells hidden away came sounds of low, sweet music.

The feast was spread upon a shell-shaped table. In the centre of the table stood the giant-kettle, Mile-deep; but so transformed that Hymir himself would not have known it. Its pearly sides gleamed with the soft tints of the rainbow, and around the edge was a rim of gold.

It had undergone a 'sea-change', and was now, indeed, 'something rich and strange'. Sea-youths and sea-maidens, some of them Ægir's own children, walked or rather floated about the palace; for in the deep sea no one walked as he would on the land.

The maidens wore robes of green, and looked like mermaids with their long hair and their crowns of gold.

The guests were seated, and the feasting began. Ægir sat at the head of the table, with Odin beside him; while Ran, his wife, sat next to Frigg.

Loki had not been invited; for, although no one could say that he had killed Baldr, all the Æsir felt that he had planned to bring about his death; and they could no longer endure his presence. But, unbidden, he appeared while they were feasting; determined to spoil their pleasure if he might not share it. He stood near the great door, looking with eyes of hate upon the fair scene. When some of the gods praised Ægir's servants, his fierce jealousy was aroused; for he could not endure to hear anyone praised. And there in the presence of Ægir and the gods he slew one of the servants. Thereupon the Æsir shook their shields and drove him from the hall. He quickly disappeared in the forest of sea-trees.

They went back to their feasting; but it was not long before Loki returned. With a sneer on his lips and fierce hatred in his eyes, he asked for a drink of the mead and a seat at the table. Bragi had great cause for disliking Loki, because he had betrayed Idunn, his wife, into the hands of Thiassi; and he spoke first:

'A seat and place will the Æsir never find for you at their board!' Loki answered him with taunts and sneers. Then he turned to Odin and reminded him of the oath they had sworn when both were young; and he told how, in those days, Odin refused even to taste beer unless it were offered to him also.

Not wishing to have the feast disturbed, Odin spoke to Vidar, the silent, and said, 'Rise, Vidar, and let the wolf's sire sit at our feast, that he may not utter insolent words in Ægir's hall.'

So Vidar rose up and presented Loki with a cup of mead; but

instead of drinking, the latter began to pour out abuse upon the gods. No one escaped his venomous tongue. And, unfortunately, many of the bitter things he said were only too true; for brave and beautiful as were the gods, few of them were pure and good like Baldr. The worst he could say of Heimdall was that he had to spend his life guarding the trembling bridge.

When he reviled Frigg, she said, 'False Loki, had I a son like Baldr here, you would not go out unhurt. You would be assaulted.'

Then, his rage and hatred making him forget caution, Loki replied, 'Shall I tell you more of my wickedness, Frigg? I am the cause of Baldr's absence. Because of me you do not see him riding to these halls.'

At these awful words the gods rose to their feet and grasped their weapons; but at a sign from Odin they restrained their wrath, and again seated themselves. No violence might be done in Ægir's halls.

Loki kept on cursing the gods until he came to Sif, Thor's wife. Thor was not there; he was far from Asgard when the Æsir were bidden to the feast. However, as Loki was abusing Sif, one of Freyja's maidens cried: 'The floor of the sea trembles. I think Thor is coming from his home. He will silence this reviler of the gods!'

She was right. In a moment a noise like thunder was heard, and Thor appeared, bearing his mighty hammer. When he understood what was going on, he called out to Loki: 'Silence, vile creature! My mighty hammer Mjöllnir shall stop your prating. I will strike your head from your neck: then your life will be ended.'

Loki's fear of Thor did not prevent his uttering insulting words to him also.

Then, again, the fierce thunder-god cried in a loud voice: 'Silence, vile creature! My mighty hammer Mjöllnir shall stop your prating. Up will I hurl you to the east region; and no one shall ever see you again!'

Still Loki would not be silenced. In a sneering tone, he said: 'Of your eastern travels you had better say little. It was there you were doubled up in a glove-thumb. You, the great hero of the gods! You hardly thought then that you were Thor.'

Thor spoke again: 'Silence, wretch! With this right hand, I, the terror of the giants, will smite you so that every bone shall be broken!'

Loki laughed a loud, mocking laugh, and said: ''Tis my intention to live a long life, although you do threaten me with your hammer. Skrymir's thongs seemed hard to you when you could not get at the food – you, strong and healthy, dying of hunger!' 'Silence, monster!' cried Thor again. 'My mighty hammer Mjöllnir shall stop your prating! I, the foe of the giants, will cast you down to hell, beneath the gratings of the dead!'

Loki spoke: 'I have said before the Æsir, and I have said before the Æsir's sons, whatever my mind suggested; but for you alone will I go out, because I know that you will fight!' Then, turning to Ægir, he said: 'Never again shall you brew beer and hold a feast of the gods. Flames shall play over all your possessions, and you shall be burnt with them!'

With these words he darted swiftly from the hall, and they saw him no more.

THE CAPTURE OF LOKI

as told by Mary Litchfield

Loki, after he had fled from Ægir's halls, hid among high mountains, and there built himself a house with four doors, which looked north, south, east and west. Near the house a stream rushed foaming over the rocks into the sea. Here he lived in constant fear of the gods; for he knew that since he had owned himself the real slayer of Baldr, they would show him no mercy. But although he had chosen the remotest and most secure hiding-place, Odin from his High Seat spied him out, and Thor and some of the other gods at once set out to capture him.

Loki knew that the gods were coming some time before they reached the house. And hastily casting a fishing-net that he was making into the fire, he changed himself into a salmon, and leaped into the neighbouring stream.

The gods entered the house, but there was no Loki. They searched, but could not find him. As they were looking carefully in every nook and corner, knowing that the crafty god possessed the power of changing himself into different shapes, one of their number noticed something peculiar in the ashes, and called the others to come and look. One said that it looked as though a device for catching fish had been recently thrust into the fire; and on pulling it out, they found that it was a half-burnt net. This suggested the idea that in order to elude them, Loki had changed himself into a fish, and had leaped into the stream nearby.

The gods at once set to work and wove a net after the pattern of the one found in the ashes; and when it was finished, they took it to the river. Putting it in, they let it sink to the bottom. And then Thor took one end, while the other gods took the other, and thus they drew it along the stream. The wily salmon, however, thrust himself between two stones and the net passed over him. So, when the gods drew it up, they found that although it had touched some living thing, there was no fish in it.

The next time they put great weights into the net, so that it raked the bed of the river. Loki, finding that he could not escape if he stayed at the bottom, and knowing that it was but a short distance to the sea, swam rapidly down the stream, and leaped over the net to where the river fell foaming over the rocks. The gods saw him as he rose above the water in his flying leap. The next time they divided themselves into two bands; and they dragged the net, while Thor followed, wading in the middle of the river. Loki must now do one of two things – leap again over the net, upstream, or swim rapidly out to sea. He chose the former course, and leaped high into the air. But Thor was ready, and with a quick motion caught him in his hand. The salmon was so slippery that he would have escaped had not Thor had a firm grip on his tail.[24] Loki was now forced to take his proper shape; and they bound him and carried him to the lower world.

In the great judgment hall near Urd's well, his doom was pronounced. All beings who had suffered through him or who knew of his crimes were called upon to testify. Frigg charged him with the death of Baldr; Bragi, with the betrayal of Idunn; and

---

24. Ever since that time salmon have had very fine, thin tails.

Skadi said that he had caused the death of her father, Thiassi. All – gods, elves, dwarfs and giants – witnessed to the harm they or their friends had suffered at the hands of the wicked god. When all the evidence was brought in, it seemed as though no punishment could be great enough for so cruel and treacherous a being.

Urd's servants took him, bound, to the dark cave near Mt Hvergelmir. And there the iron gates were opened, and they went down to the world of darkness. Torches shed their lurid light upon the awful scenes. Here were confined many horrible monsters – giants, witches and dragons – foes to gods and men.

After a long journey they reached the borders of a dark, sluggish sea. Taking a boat, they rowed out to a rocky island, rising in the midst of the sea. The island was full of caves in which monsters were confined; in one was the wolf, Fenrir. They placed Loki near his offspring, binding his feet and hands with strong chains, and fastening him firmly to the rocks. The rest of his punishment was too dreadful to be told; but dreadful as it was, Loki deserved it all.

Near the rocky island was moored an enormous ship, called *Nagelfar*; it was larger even than *Ringhorn*, Baldr's ship. When Ragnarök, the Twilight of the Gods, should come, Loki would be freed from his fetters; and gathering the hosts of evil, would set sail upon this ship to fight against the gods. Then the fierce venom of his soul, nursed through long years, would flame out in deeds against his hated foes.

THE BEGINNING OF POETRY

as told by Sarah Powers Bradish

I. KVASIR

The gods once had a great dispute with the *vanas*, the spirits of the sea and air. When peace was made, the gods created a wonderful being in honour of the event. They called him Kvasir.

Kvasir was very wise, almost as wise as Odin himself. He spent his time walking up and down the earth, answering the questions of men. He taught new and useful things. Men loved him because he was so good and kind.

The dwarfs were jealous of him, and sought to destroy him. One day two dwarfs, Fialar and Galar, came upon him as he lay asleep in the forest, and killed him. They found his charm and saved it. It was a liquid, which they mixed with honey, to make a kind of mead. They kept it in three vessels: the kettle Odhoerir (inspiration), the bowl Son (expiation) and the cup Boden (offering). They knew that whoever tasted this magic mead would instantly become a poet, a sweet singer or an orator. Still, none of the dwarfs ever touched the mead. They kept it hidden in a secret place.

One day the dwarfs found the giant, Gilling, asleep on a steep bank. They shoved him off into the water, and he was drowned. Then the wicked dwarfs rolled a millstone upon the roof of Gilling's house. Some of them went into the house and told the giantess that her husband was dead. Frantic with grief, she rushed out to find his body. Just as she left the door, the other dwarfs rolled the stone down upon her head, and crushed her.

The cruel dwarfs thought themselves safe, because Gilling had no children to avenge his death. But he had a brother, Suttung, who caught them, and placed them on a shoal, where the tide would be sure to carry them out to sea. They begged for their lives, but he was deaf to their entreaties, until they promised to give him their precious mead. Then he took them back to the shore, and they brought him the kettle Odhoerir, the bowl Son and the cup Boden. He gave them to his daughter, Gunlod, at the same time forbidding her to give a taste to either gods or men.

Gunlod watched over her charge day and night. To guard it more securely, she carried it into a cave within a mountain. Even Odin would hardly have known where it was, but for his ever-watchful ravens, Hugin and Munin, who flew back to Asgard with the news as soon as Gunlod had found a place for her treasure.

II. ODIN WORKS ON A FARM

Odin was very wise, because, ages before, he had exchanged one of his eyes for a drink from Mimir's well at the foot of the great world tree, Yggdrasil. He had also hung nine days and nine nights from the boughs of Yggdrasil, for the sake of mastering the magic runes. But he was not a poet, and he could not sing. He could not rest until he had tasted the mead of the dwarfs. He put on his cloud cloak and his broad-brimmed hat, and set out for the land of the giants.

On the way to the house of Suttung, he passed a meadow where nine thralls were mowing. Their scythes were very dull. He drew a whetstone from the folds of his cloak and offered to sharpen them. The thralls gladly accepted his service.

He did the work so quickly and so well that they asked to be allowed to keep the whetstone. Odin tossed it up in the air toward them. In the scramble that followed, the thralls became entangled in their scythes in such a way that each one cut off his neighbour's head. Odin, not at all disturbed, went quietly on his way.

He soon came to the house of Baugi, a brother of Suttung. Baugi received him very kindly. During their conversation, the giant said he did not know how he was going to finish haying, because all his thralls had been killed.

Odin at once offered to do the work of the nine thralls, if, at the end of the season, Baugi would get for him one draught of Suttung's mead. This, Baugi agreed to do; and Odin, who had given his name as Bolwerk, went to work. The hay was secured, the grain harvested, and all the summer work of the farm finished before the autumn rains set in.

When the first days of winter came, Bolwerk went to his master to ask for the prompt payment of his wages. Baugi said he dared not ask his brother for the mead, but he would try to get a few drops of it as he had promised.

III. GUNLOD'S TREASURE

Odin and Baugi went together to the mountain where Gunlod was hidden. They could find no entrance to her cave. Odin gave Baugi his auger, Roti, and told him to bore a hole, through which they could creep into the mountain.

Baugi worked for a few minutes, and said he had bored the hole. Odin, suspecting treachery, blew into the hole. Dust and chips flew back into his face, so that he knew the hole did not reach clear through the rock. He told Baugi to bore again. When he blew into the hole a second time, no dust came back; and he knew an opening had been made into the cave. He took the form of a worm and crawled through the hole. Treacherous Baugi thrust the auger in after him, hoping to crush him, but he had come out on the other side.

Odin at once resumed his own form, and asked Gunlod for a sip of the mead. Three days and three nights he begged, but Gunlod refused.

At last, she brought out the three vessels, and told him he might take a little from each. But Odin managed to get every drop of the precious mead. Then he became an eagle, and flew away over the mountain tops toward Asgard. His flight was slow, on account of the weight of the mead. He was still a long way from Asgard, when he found that he was pursued. Suttung had also put on eagle's plumage, and was fast overtaking him. But Odin strained every muscle, and reached the wall a little in advance of Suttung.

The gods had seen the race, and had gathered a pile of chips and shavings, which they set on fire, just as Suttung flew over the wall. The flames rose high in the air, and burned the wings of Suttung, who fell into the fire and was destroyed.

Odin flew to the urn, which had been prepared to receive the mead, and poured it out with such haste that a few drops fell on the earth. Men found it, and as many as possible tasted it. All who tasted were known as rhymesters and poetasters.

The gods carefully preserved the mead; and sometimes, at long intervals, they gave a little to some favoured man, whom they wished to become famous for poetry or eloquence.

But Odin sipped only a little of the mead. Most of it was kept for his son, Bragi, who was born about this time. Bragi became the god of poetry and music. The gods gave him a magic golden harp, and put him into a ship, and let him sail over the ocean.

As the ship floated along, Bragi took the harp, and sang the 'Song of Life', the sound of which rose to Asgard, and fell to the abode of Hela. As he played and sang, the ship glided over the water, and touched the shore. The young god walked through the forest, playing and singing as he went. The trees budded and blossomed, and flowers sprang up in the grass along his path, within the sound of the music.

In the forest he met Idunn, the daughter of Ivald, the dwarf. Idunn became Bragi's wife and the goddess of flowers and of immortal youth.

THE JUDGMENT HALL OF THE DEAD

as told by Sarah Powers Bradish

Each day Odin and the other gods rode over Bifröst, going towards the south, and went down to the lower world. Near the southern end of the celestial bridge was the well that watered the third root of Yggdrasil. An old book says that the waters of this well were so 'holy that everything that is put in the well becomes as white as the membrane between the egg and the eggshell'. The roots of Yggdrasil were continually sprinkled with its waters, and were as white as silver in consequence. Two swans of purest white, the parents of all the swans that ever have been, glided over its surface; and its edge, like that of Mimir's well, was thickly overlaid with gold.

Urd, the great norn who was queen of the world of the dead, dwelt near the well with her two sisters. Multitudes of messengers and attendants stood ready to do her bidding; for her realms were vast, her power extending even to the dark region under Niflheim. All beings who died in Midgard came first to the great judgment hall near her well. And it was to meet them there, and with Urd to pass judgment upon them, that the gods each day crossed the trembling bridge and came to the lower world. Thor, the thunder-god, could not pass over the bridge, because his heavy iron chariot would have injured it; so he was obliged to ford three rivers on his way.

The great judgment hall was a solemn place, and the decisions pronounced there, whether gentle or severe, were always just.

Mortals who had been very wicked were sent to the world of torture. Those who had died on the field of battle were claimed by Odin, the All-Father, or by Freyja, a Van-goddess who lived in Asgard with the Æsir. Odin sent his maidens, the Valkyries, to choose the heroes on the battlefield, and to conduct them to Asgard. They went to his great palace of Valhalla; and there they feasted and fought each day, that they might be ready to do battle with the powers of evil when Ragnarök, the Twilight of the Gods, should come.[25] Freyja united again lovers who had been faithful unto death. Mortals whose lives had been peaceful and pure went to a home prepared for them by Urd, in a land where the fields stretched green and beautiful, and where it was always summer.

---

25. Freyr's sister, a Van-goddess. Half of the slain in battle belonged to her.

THE TWILIGHT OF THE GODS

as told by Mary Litchfield

When the gods returned to Asgard, it seemed to them that everything was changed. Baldr was gone forever, and Loki, once a gay, witty companion, and later a secret and dreaded foe, was securely bound in the world of darkness. As evening fell upon the city, Odin, surrounded by the greater gods, stood looking out upon the sea, over which the ship *Ringhorn* had borne the dead Baldr.

All were silent, until at last Odin spoke: 'Baldr has gone, and Loki is punished. A new life begins; and it is right that you, the wisest and strongest of the Æsir, should know what lies before you, and before us all. You are strong, and can bear the truth, hard though it be. You have heard that a time is coming, called the Twilight of the Gods; it is of that I will now speak.' Then silence reigned again, while Odin stood with bowed head.

At last he spoke, uttering this solemn prophecy, while his eyes seemed looking into the far, dim future:

'As the ages roll on, wickedness shall increase in Asgard, and in the world of men. Witches and monsters shall be bred up in the iron-wood, and shall sow the seeds of evil in the world. Brothers shall slay each other; cousins shall violate kinship; shields shall be cloven; no man will spare another. Hard shall it be in the world – an axe age, a sword age, a wind age, ere the world sinks.

'The great Fimbul winter shall come, when snow shall fall from the four corners of heaven; deadly will be the frosts, and piercing the winds, and the darkened sun will impart no gladness. Three such winters shall come, and no summer to gladden the heart with sunshine. Then shall follow more winters, when even greater discord shall prevail. Fierce wolves shall devour the sun and moon, and the stars shall fall from heaven. The earth shall tremble, the stony hills shall be dashed together, giants shall totter, and dwarfs groan before their stony doors. Men shall seek the paths leading to the realms of death; and earth, in flames, shall sink beneath the seething ocean.

'Then shall the aged World Tree tremble; and loudly shall bark the dog of hell. At that sound shall the fetters of Loki and the wolf be broken; and the Midgard serpent, with terrible lashing and struggling, shall forsake the sea. The ship *Nagelfar* shall be loosed from its moorings by the rocky isle; and all the hosts of evil shall go on board, while Loki steers them across the sluggish sea. Surt[26] shall leave his fiery dales, and join the hosts of evil, to fight against the gods.

'Loudly shall the ancient horn of Heimdall then resound throughout the nine worlds. And when they hear the sound, the hosts of Odin shall make ready; the gods and all the warriors of Valhalla shall buckle on their armour for the last great fight. Odin shall seek wisdom from Mimir, that he may know how best to meet his foes.

---

26. Surt was the father of Suttung, from whom Odin treacherously obtained the poetic mead – the mead that could make men poets.

27. This plain was a hundred miles square.

'Terrible will be the onset when on the great plain[27] the hosts of the sons of destruction meet the armies of the gods. Then will come the second grief to Frigg, when Odin goes to meet the wolf. For then will her beloved fall. But Vidar, the great son of Odin, shall pierce the heart of Loki's offspring, and avenge his father's death. Mighty Thor will meet the Midgard serpent, and in his rage will slay the worm. Back nine paces will he go, and then fall – he who feared no foe – slain by the venom of the deadly beast. Tyr shall meet the fierce dog of hell, and they shall slay each other. Freyr will meet his death at the hand of Surt, slain by Thiassi's fatal sword. Little shall the love of Gerd avail him on that day. Heimdall, the wise and pure, shall fall at the hand of Loki, the father of monsters, and shall in turn cause Loki's death. Few shall be left alive who meet in that great fight!'

He ceased, and there was silence, while the shadows deepened, and the sea grew dark.

Finally Tyr spoke: 'And is there no hope, Odin? Does all end in darkness?' At these words Odin's face changed; a gleam of sunshine seemed to fall upon it, and he said: 'I see arise, a second time, earth from ocean, beauteously green. I see waterfalls where leap the fish, and eagles flying over the hills. I see Baldr and Hodur, the rulers of a purer race of mortals – mortals who have long served Baldr in the lower world – and near them Vidar and the sons of Thor. They meet on Ida's plains, and call to memory the mighty deeds of the old gods, and their ancient lore. They speak of the serpent, the great earth-encircler, and of the deeds of Loki and of Thor. Unsown shall the fields bring forth, and all evil shall be done away with, when Baldr and Hodur reign.'

He ceased, while his gaze seemed penetrating through the misty ages.

The silence was long; but finally one of the gods said: 'And what of us, Odin? Is there no hope for the old gods?'

As he spoke, a look never before seen on his bold features overspread the face of Odin, and raising his eyes reverently, he said: 'After the Twilight of the Gods shall come the Mighty One to judgment – He whom we dare not name, the powerful One from above, who rules over all. He shall dooms pronounce, and strifes allay, and holy peace establish, which shall be forevermore. I see a hall with gold bedecked, brighter than the sun, standing in the high heavens. There shall the righteous dwell forevermore, in peace and happiness.'

As the vision faded, Odin looked upon the gods, who stood silent before him. 'My children,' said the All-Father, 'let us be strong and valiant. Long will be the ages, hard will be the fighting, and many the woes that we must endure; but the brave heart loves danger, and the strong soul shrinks not from evil and sorrow. To do our best, knowing that we shall fail; to fight to the end, and then give place to those who are wholly pure and good – that is the fate of the old gods. He whom we may not name has so decreed it; and His decrees are ever just and right.'

TALES FROM THE SAGAS

THE STORY OF VÖLUND

as told by by Julia Goddard

There was once a king of Finnland who had three sons, all eager lovers of hunting. The two elder were named Slagfin and Egil, the youngest was called Völund.

But Völund not only loved hunting like his brothers; he had a power which his brothers did not possess. He was a wonderful craftsman at the forge, and could make arrow-heads, spears and weapons of all kinds. Moreover, he could model shields with rare chasing, and sometimes would fashion chains and armlets of fine gold that the daintiest queen might be proud to wear.

So well he loved his work that he spent more than half his time at the forge, and never gave it up but for a day's hunting with his brothers. And more than once he even gave up the chase, for though he loved hunting well, he loved his anvil better. And his workshop was quite a sight to see with all the wonderful things that he had made hanging round.

At last Slagfin said to Egil, 'Völund spends too much of his time at the forge, it is not work befitting a king's son. He will lose all interest in the chase, unless something is done to rouse him.'

And Egil replied: 'Thou hast spoken well, my brother, and a thought has come into my mind. I am growing tired of the hunting grounds near home; the sport is not so good as it used to be. But far away in Ulfdal, on the shores of Ulf lake, is a mighty forest. There we may chase the wolf and the wild boar, and in the lake we may catch more fish than we shall know what to do with. Let us go thither and take Völund with us. Then will he forget his forge and his bellows, and live as a king's son ought to live.'

The idea pleased Slagfin greatly, and away he went to Völund to propose the plan. He found Völund at work upon slender spears of a new pattern.

'Ha!' he said, as he took one of them up to look at. 'We could make good use of this at Ulfdal. What do you say to going there with Egil and myself? We might build a hut on the borders of the lake, and live upon the game we kill. You have been toiling at your forge too long, the change will do you good.'

'I must finish this spear first,' returned Völund. 'It is the best of the lot, and though it is so light, it is so strong that nothing can blunt its point or break it in twain.'

'Work away, then,' said Slagfin, 'but be ready to start with Egil and me by tomorrow's dawn. You must bring your choicest weapons with you, for we expect rare sport.'

'Take any you please,' answered Völund, 'for I have no time to choose for you. The spear I am working upon will suffice for me, I shall want no other weapon.'

Then Slagfin chose arrows, and sharp spears, and hooks, and strong chains, long nails and a heavy hammer.

'We must build for ourselves,' he said, 'for no man dwells on the borders of Ulf lake.'

'So much the better,' responded Völund; 'I like the sound of my hammer, and the song of the birds, better than the voices of men.'

And Slagfin went away well pleased that Völund was willing to go to Ulfdal. And early in the morning, just as the sun was rising over the low hills, the three brothers were seen loaded with their hunting gear, starting off for the wild forest that bordered the lake.

Völund was strong and mighty of limb; he had muscles almost as strong as those of Thor, his eyes were dark, and his black hair curled crisply round his brow. He was not so handsome as his fair-headed brothers, but he was taller and more like a king, and everyone said as he passed along, 'There is no one in Finnland to equal Völund.'

Further and further they left the city behind, wilder grew the country and the sun shone high above them.

'Shall we not rest?' asked Egil. 'We have journeyed many a mile and my limbs are weary; besides, it will be pleasanter travelling when the sun goes down.'

Then Völund smiled: 'If you were accustomed as I am to the heat of the forge, you would not mind the sun's rays. Nevertheless, let it be as you please,' he added, throwing himself down at the foot of a tall pine tree. 'There is no hurry for getting to Ulfdal, the game will not chide our loitering, since it will give them longer life in the forest.'

So the three brothers rested and after a while set out again on their march. There remained yet three days' journey to Ulfdal. But at length they reached it, and were repaid for their toil when they saw the tall pines shoot up their branches high into the air, and heard the low growl of the wolf not far off, and beheld the blue lake stretching out like a quiet sea with the wild swan sailing on its glassy waters and the water-fowl rustling among the reeds and rushes.

'This is a pleasant place,' quoth Slagfin.

Then the brothers heaped together a pile of boughs and brushwood and made themselves a fire. And Egil fitted an arrow to his bow and shot the sea-fowl as they lazily fluttered by, whilst Slagfin cast a net into the lake and hauled up a plentiful supply of fish.

Meanwhile the strong Völund had cut down several pines and built up a hut so quickly that Slagfin and Egil thought it had been done by magic.

It was but a rude hovel for the sons of a king, but what did the princes care? The summer sun shone brightly and the nights were warm, and besides they loved hunting well enough to care little for all discomforts.

They spent their time in the forest, and many a wolf-skin would they have to carry back to Finnland. Many a wild boar fell under the spear of Völund, and there was great slaughter among the water-fowl and the wild deer.

Day after day went by, and Völund rejoiced so much in the great free forest that Slagfin and Egil hoped that he had forgotten his forge.

One morning when they went forth from the hut they marvelled at hearing voices in the distance; and not the voices of men, but low sweet tones and gentle laughter, such as they were accustomed to hear from the queen's ladies at court.

And lo, close by the water's edge there sat three fair maidens spinning flax. And as they span they sang a song that even to Völund sounded sweeter than the notes of the forest birds.

The brothers drew nearer, and never had they seen faces so fair as those of the three maidens, who were so busily engaged in their task that they did not see Völund and his brothers until they were close to them.

When however they did see them, they seemed in no whit abashed, but began to talk to them, and to tell them how they too had heard of the quiet Ulf lake and had determined to leave their own country and abide on the outskirts of the wild forest.

'So we put on our swan-coats and flew away,' said the maidens, 'and the king, our father, knows not what has become of us.'

When Slagfin heard that the damsels were king's daughters he was very glad, for he had already fallen in love with one of them. So also had Egil, and so even had Völund, and by good luck each had chosen a different princess. There was no need of quarrelling in the matter, and it was soon arranged that the three princes should marry the three princesses and that they should all remain in Ulfdal together.

For a long time everything went well, and they were all very happy, and Völund and his brothers would have been content to live for ever in the forest with their beautiful wives. They went out hunting together, and Völund had built up a forge and he made all sorts of ornaments for his wife and her sisters.

But it happened that the sisters grew tired of the life they were leading. Though Völund and his brothers did not know it, their wives were Valkyries, who loved war better than anything else, and so they became weary of the pleasures of hunting and longed to go to battle again. And one day when their husbands were absent they put on their swan-coats and flew away.

When the brothers came back and found that their wives had left them they were in great trouble, and Slagfin and Egil determined to stay no longer in Ulfdal, but to seek through the world for their lost princesses. But Völund resolved to stay where he was, hoping that perchance his wife might come back to him; and he continued to make armlets and necklaces and delicate chains to please her when she should return. But alas, she never came back.

And after a time it came to pass that Nidad, King of Sweden, heard tell of Völund and how he could make all sorts of armour and weapons and trinkets. And Nidad sent a band of armed men to Ulfdal, who took Völund and brought him to Sweden.

There he was obliged to work at the forge for the king's pleasure, and to make swords of sharpness and shoes of swiftness, and other marvels for the king and his people. And Völund was very angry and several times sought to escape.

Then the queen counselled Nidad to cut the sinews of Völund's legs, so that he should be unable to walk and might remain with them always.

And when this was done Völund was put on the island of Sjoa-stad, where he was obliged to work day and night with scarcely any rest.

Völund was very wroth at being thus cruelly treated, and determined upon revenging himself; but it was a long time before he was able to do so. He was lame and could not move about, and he grew very weary and began to languish. At last two of the king's sons came to him, and with bitter taunts bade him make two swords, sharper than any he had yet made; and Völund's wrath was roused yet more, and he rose up and slew the two young men, and of their skulls he made drinking cups which he sent to the king, and of their teeth a breast jewel for the queen. And the king and queen admired them greatly, little knowing how they had been made.

Soon the king's sons were missed, and search was made for them, but they were not to be found.

Long mourned the king and the queen; but Völund kept his secret, and worked on at the forge.

One fine morning when he was toiling at a shield which the king had bidden him make, the king's only daughter came to ask him to make a ring and a chain of gold for her.

She was very fair, fairer even than his Valkyrie wife, and she spoke in a gentle tone to Völund, for she felt the more sorry that he had to work so hard, because she knew he was the son of a king. And Völund gazed eagerly upon her, and her soft voice was like music to his heart. He promised to make a ring and a chain of gold more beautiful than any she had ever seen, and the princess went away well pleased, promising to come for them in two days.

The two days seemed very long to the princess, for she was eager to see what her ring would be like, and she wanted to see Völund again, for she pitied him greatly.

To Völund the time went more quickly, for he had work to do, and the chain and the ring were only just made when the princess came for them.

She was delighted when she saw them, for never had anything been so delicately wrought in Sweden.

And Völund threw the chain around her neck, and gently put the ring on her finger, and then he sighed.

'Why do you sigh?' asked the princess.

'For my sorrows,' replied Völund.

'Ah, you wish to go back to your own land,' said the princess; 'I do not wonder at it, for it is sad to be a captive.'

'Until two days since I wished to return,' answered Völund, 'but not now unless, indeed,' he added, 'you would go with me and be Queen of Finnland.'

The princess made no answer, but Völund knew that she was not angry, for there was a smile upon her lips.

And after she was gone, Völund began to work away at something that he had not thought of before, and that was not in the way of his trade. He made two coats of feathers, so light that they would rise into the air of themselves; and the next time that the princess came he asked again if she would fly away with him and be Queen of Finnland.

Still the princess made no answer, but she took a ring from her hand and gave it to Völund and then went away, and Völund knew that before long he should fly home to his own country.

Again came the princess and again Völund asked her if she would fly away with him and be Queen of Finnland.

And the princess took up one of the feather coats, and without saying a word drew it over her dress. Then Völund put on the other coat and they rose up high into the air.

King Nidad and his queen were sitting on the terrace in front of the palace when Völund and the beautiful princess floated by.

The king shouted loudly, 'Ah, traitor! Thou art carrying away my daughter. Out, archers, out and shoot him.'

And Völund answered: 'I have revenged myself for thy cruelty to me. Thy sons have I slain, and from their skulls hast thou drunk the sparkling wine, and the queen wears their teeth in her shining breast jewel. And now do I take thy daughter from thee, since she loves me better than she loves thee.'

Then higher, higher rose Völund and the princess into the air, and soon they were out of sight.

There were great rejoicings in Finnland when Völund alighted at the palace, for the old king was dead, and Slagfin and Egil had not yet come home from searching after their wives, and the people had no one to reign over them.

So Völund reigned over Finnland, and ruled his people wisely and well. Nevertheless he loved his forge better than ruling, and all his spare time he worked away at his smithy, and may be working there yet if one could only tell where to find him.

KING OLAF THE SAINT

as told by Julia Goddard

Hundreds of years ago lived Olaf, a brave king, and his brother Harald Haardrade.

One day, when these brothers were talking together, they began to speak of old Norroway, the land of their birth.

'It is a land full of high hills,' said one.

'It is a land full of fertile valleys,' said the other, 'where there is no lack of waving corn, fair pastures and summer flowers.'

'It is a land over which anyone might be content to reign,' said Olaf; 'a monarch might be justly proud of such a kingdom.'

'Truly,' replied Harald Haardrade; 'better fortune could no man wish.'

'Then,' answered Olaf, 'let us make a bargain. Our ships are in the harbour; they are well matched. Let us sail forth, and he who reaches first our native land shall be king of old Norroway.'

'I am quite willing,' said Harald Haardrade; 'yet there is one condition I should like to make. Thou hast said that our ships are equally matched; nevertheless, I take thine to be the fastest sailer. Art thou willing to change vessels with me? So will we run the race.'

'I am willing,' said Olaf. 'If thou thinkest my vessel to be the fleeter, take her, and welcome, and I will take thine. Is this a fair bargain?'

'Perfectly fair,' answered Harald Haardrade, well satisfied that he should have his brother's ship.

Now the vessel belonging to Olaf was called the *Dragon*. Lightly she danced over the waves, and a child could have turned her north, south, east or west, by just one touch to the rudder. Harald Haardrade's ship, the *Ox*, was heavier built, and not so easy to manage; nevertheless, there was no fault to be found with her.

However, Olaf thought one vessel as good as the other, and, therefore, said nought against his brother's proposal; perhaps, too, he felt himself to be the better seaman. However this may have been, the story does not say; but there is reason to think that something in his heart told Olaf that the change of ships would make no difference to their captains.

So the brothers parted, and Olaf, having made all things ready, went to the church to pray for a blessing upon his work, 'For', said he, 'how can I expect to prosper unless I have the blessing of heaven?'

And as he passed along the aisle of the stately building, with his beautiful hair flowing over his shoulders, the people wished him success, and prayed that good King Olaf might win the race. As he moved along in solemn mood, a messenger came in hot haste, and stopped him, saying, 'Why dost thou waste time, King Olaf? Thy brother is sailing away in the *Dragon*. Far ahead of thee will he be, if thou dost not turn thy steps aside from the altar, and follow him without delay.'

But King Olaf answered the messenger, 'Let those sail who choose to sail; I will not depart without the blessing of heaven.'

And so he waited quietly until the mass was over, and then went calmly down to the seashore. The great white-crested waves were dashing on the strand, and the *Ox* rocked heavily at her moorings, and over the wide sweep of blue sea there was no sign of the *Dragon*. Away, far away, had the *Dragon* sped; the wind was in her favour, and she had weighed anchor, and set her sails, and danced gallantly away till there were now many miles between her and the shore. Olaf strained his eyes, and saw a speck of white that fluttered for a moment and then vanished. Perchance it might be the *Dragon*.

However, Olaf did not despair. He had asked the blessing of heaven upon his undertaking, and although the beginning seemed bad, yet he said in his heart, 'Who can see so far as the end? I will not be dismayed.'

Strong in the might of his faith, he bade the sailors get ready, and when all was done he stepped on board his vessel. The anchor was raised; a gentle breeze stirred the sails; the helmsman guided the ship seaward; and as King Olaf stood at the prow, he said reverently, 'O *Ox*, *Ox*, speed thee on in the Name of the Lord.'

Then he leaned forward, and taking hold of one of the white horns of the *Ox*, as though it had been a living creature, he said, 'Now speed thee, O thou patient *Ox*, even as though thou wert going to pasture in fragrant clover fields.'

And as if in answer to his words, the heavy vessel gave a leap, and gallantly ploughed the wild waves. And the white spray rose even until it frosted over the king's beautiful locks, and he shouted to the watcher on the topmost mast, 'Ho, lad! Ho! Canst thou see aught of the fleet-sailing *Dragon*?'

And the lad answered, 'I see naught upon the sea. There is not even a fishing-boat out upon the broad waters.'

And on they sailed in silence. After a while, King Olaf called to the lad again, 'Ho, lad! Ho! Canst thou see aught of the good ship *Dragon*?' Then the lad answered, 'Nigh the land of Norroway I espy the silken sails of a vessel. The sun shines upon them, and they glitter as though they were bordered with gold.'

And King Olaf knew that it was his own brave ship, and again they sailed on in silence. After a while he called yet again to the lad, 'Ho, lad! Ho! Canst thou see aught of the *Dragon*?' And the lad made answer, 'Nigh the shores of old Norroway, under the shade of the purple mountains, I see a vessel riding full sail before the wind, and I know that it is the good ship *Dragon*.'

Then King Olaf struck the *Ox* upon the ribs, and cried, 'Faster, faster, thou *Ox*, faster. There is no time to lose.'

And again he struck the Ox upon the eye, and shouted, 'Faster, faster, faster, if thou wouldst have me win the haven.'

And suddenly it seemed as though the *Ox* had started into life, and was putting forth all its new-gained powers, for forward bounded the vessel with a sudden leap. Swiftly, swiftly, swiftly, no one had ever known such sailing. Swifter than a bird on the wing, swifter than an arrow through the air. So sped the *Ox* through the foaming sea. The sailors could not climb the rigging; indeed, it was more than they could do to stand firmly upon the deck; so King Olaf lashed them firmly to the masts, though the steersman asked him who was going to guide the ship. 'I will see to that myself,' answered King Olaf; 'not one of you shall be lost through me. I will guide the ship straight on like a line of light.' And King Olaf stood by the helm, and he steered neither to the right nor to the left, but on, straight on, and his eye was fixed upon the goal.

'So must I run,' he said, 'if I would win the race.'

What mattered it to King Olaf though rocks and mountains stood in the way? His faith was stronger than the rocks. Right onward he went, and the valleys filled with water, and the mountains disappeared, the blue waves rolled over them, and the *Ox* went triumphantly on its way. Out came running the little elves, for the sudden rising of the floods had disturbed them. 'Who art thou, bold mariner, who sailest over our homes? Behold the mountains shake with fury. Tell us what is thy name?'

'Quiet ye, quiet ye, little people,' answered King Olaf. 'I am Saint Olaf; turn ye into stones until I come this way again.'

So the little elves turned into stones, and rolled down the mountain sides, and the good ship went on her way. She had not gone far before out came an old Carline, and said, 'Saint Olaf, I know you, with your beard shining like red gold. Wherefore do you bring with you the waters to mock us in our dwellings? Your ship has burst through the wall of my chamber. Evil luck be with you.'

Then Saint Olaf, for he was a saint as well as a king, fixed his glance witheringly upon the old Carline.

'Be thou turned into a flint rock,' said he, 'and so remain for ever and ever.'

And the Carline was turned into a rock, and Saint Olaf and his crew sailed on and on. So fleetly flew the good ship *Ox*, that anyone must have had good eyes to see her as she flashed past, for so she sped on that if Saint Olaf drew his bow and shot an arrow forward, it fell far behind in the wake of the vessel.

This was fast sailing indeed, and with such speed it is not wonderful that though Harald Haardrade had had the start of his brother, yet Saint Olaf reached home three days before him. Harald Haardrade was wild with rage when he came those three days later and found Saint Olaf king of Norroway. And he raged and raged until at length he became a dragon. And this is the last that we hear of Harald Haardrade.

Now, as Saint Olaf had prayed for the blessing of heaven before he set out on his voyage, it was natural that his first act upon landing should be to go to the nearest church to return thanks for having so mightily prospered. And as he walked up the crowded nave, a golden glory beamed from his fair hair, and the people of Norroway learned a great lesson from the faith of King Olaf the Saint.

KING SIGMUND

as told by Sarah Powers Bradish

I. HELGI

Sigmund gathered an army, and all embarked on ships, to go back to his native land. Sinfiotli was his constant assistant and adviser. When they arrived at the land of the Völsungs, the people received them gladly, and proclaimed Sigmund king.

When he sat once more beneath the Branstock, he thought of Signy, and how she had given herself to save her father's family; and he remembered her wedding day, when he had drawn the sword of Odin from the oak; and how he had thought, that day, that he might be left to defend the Branstock, after his father and brothers had ascended to the halls of Odin.

He married a princess, whose name was Borghild.

They had two sons, named Hamond and Helgi. When Helgi lay in the cradle, the Norns entered the room, and blessed the newborn babe. They called him 'Sunlit Hill', 'Sharp Sword' and 'Lord of Rings'; and promised him a glorious career. He was brought up in the house of Hagal, a wise teacher.

At the age of fifteen, he had grown so tall, and had become so brave, that he ventured alone into the house of Hunding, his father's enemy. The family did not recognize the young prince; and he passed through without exciting much attention. But he left an insolent message, which made Hunding so angry that he started in pursuit of the bold young fellow. Hunding followed him to Hagal's house, and went in after him; but found no one, except a maid, who was grinding corn. Hunding was surprised that a maid should be so tall, and have such brawny arms; but he did not suspect that she was Helgi, in disguise, as she really was.

After this, Helgi was considered proficient enough, in courage and cunning, to join the army. He marched, with Sinfiotli, against the Hundings, and fought a great battle. The Valkyries were hovering near, waiting to choose the slain for Odin's halls, when their attention was called to the great courage of Helgi. One of their number, named Gudrun, admired him so much that she came to him and offered to be his wife. They were married at once.

After the battle, only one of the Hunding family remained alive; and he was allowed to go free, after he had promised not to avenge the death of his father; but he borrowed Odin's spear, and killed Helgi. Helgi's wife was heartbroken at the death of her husband. She wept constantly, until she learned that, every day, Helgi's voice called to her from his tomb. That night, she entered the tomb, and asked why Helgi called her, and why his wounds still bled. Helgi's voice answered, 'I cannot be happy while you weep; and, for every tear you shed, a drop of my blood must flow.'

Gudrun wept no more; but Odin soon called her, to cross the rainbow bridge. Helgi had been made leader of the heroes in Valhalla; and Gudrun, again a Valkyr, came to earth, to choose the slain heroes, who should fight under Helgi's command at the last great battle.

II. SINFIOTLI AND GUDROD

After the death of Helgi, Sinfiotli returned to Sigmund's palace, where he was held in high esteem. But he soon became weary of continual feasting and song, and longed for an active life. In the spring, he joined his forces to those of Gudrod, Borghild's brother, and sailed over the sea, to gain new victories.

They conquered a rich nation, and took much spoil. Gudrod was brave in battle, but he had a greedy heart. He wanted to divide the spoil at once; but Sinfiotli said it was not becoming, in two kings of war, to dispute over booty, as pirates might do; and that he would come back at night, and take what Gudrod thought best to give him. He went to his warship, to rest until evening.

Gudrod worked all day; and, when Sinfiotli returned at night, he found the spoil divided into two parts, and Sinfiotli's share was larger than Gudrod's. But the things of value were all in Gudrod's part. Sinfiotli was indignant; and the men of his command were very angry. Gudrod, seeing this discontent, called on his own men to slay the 'wood abider'; but the soldiers stood still, and no sword was unsheathed.

Then Sinfiotli challenged Gudrod to single combat, and they met the next morning. Gudrod fought bravely, but fell mortally wounded.

Sinfiotli returned to the land of the Völsungs, with the army. Sigmund made a feast in his honour, and was listening to the story of the war, when Borghild entered and asked why her brother had not come back from the sea. Sinfiotli answered:

'The white swords met in the island; bright there did the war shields shine. And there thy brother abideth; for his hand was worse than mine.'

Borghild called on Sigmund to drive this 'wolf of the kingfolk' out of the land of the Völsungs.

Sigmund answered that, when she had heard the story of the war, she would know that her brother had not kept his word. But, even if he had stood by his agreement, Sinfiotli could not be punished, because Gudrod had perished in a fair fight. Still he said that he would pay gold for her brother's death, because he loved her.

Borghild went to her own apartments, where she lay silent for a long time.

III. THE DEATH OF SINFIOTLI

The next day Borghild went to Sigmund to say that she was no longer angry, and that she would take his gold. She kissed him and Sinfiotli also, and sat down on the high-seat. She asked her husband to make a funeral feast for her brother, Gudrod. This he was willing to do, and one autumn evening all the princes and earls assembled in the great hall under the Branstock to do honour to Gudrod's memory. Borghild was there, and pouring wine for Sinfiotli, said, 'Drink now of the cup from my hand, and let us bury hate that is dead.'

Sinfiotli took the cup, but did not drink.

Sigmund asked why he sat so silent and sorrowful in the midst of the feast.

Sinfiotli said that he saw hate in the cup.

'Give it to me,' answered Sigmund, and taking the cup, he drank the wine.

Borghild gave Sinfiotli another cup, which he passed to

Sigmund, who drank as before. When she brought the third cup, she taunted Sinfiotli with cowardice and fear of death. He took the cup from her hand, but did not drink. Sigmund again asked why he took no part in the feast, and he said, 'Because there is death in the cup.'

The old king did not take the wine this time, and Sinfiotli thought that he wished him to drink it. So he raised it to his lips, and drained the cup, and fell back dead.

Sigmund raised the body of his foster son. His grief was so great that no one dared look upon it, or listen to the words he spoke. He bore the body in his arms out into the darkness. The wind shrieked through the Branstock, and blew black clouds across the face of the moon. Sigmund went away from the dwellings of men to the forest at the foot of the mountains. A wide river stopped his progress. He followed along its bank until he came to the sea. An ancient, one-eyed boatman hailed him, and asked where he was going. He answered that he wished to cross the sea, because the light of his life had gone out.

'I have come', said the boatman, 'to convey a great king across the water.'

So Sigmund laid the body in the bottom of the boat; but before he could himself step in, the boat and the boatman had vanished. Then he knew that the boatman was Odin, and that he had taken Sinfiotli to the home of the heroes.

IV. THE DEATH OF SIGMUND

Sigmund went back to his father's throne, and attended to the business of the kingdom. He went to war and conquered his enemies; but he cared little for glory, now that Sinfiotli and Helgi were gone. He had sent Borghild away after Sinfiotli's death, and he was left alone in the great house of the Völsungs.

He heard that a distant king had a daughter who was beautiful, good and wise; and he sent an earl laden with gold and gifts, to ask her to be his queen. The king's name was Eylimi, and his daughter's name was Hiordis.

On the very day of the earl's arrival at Eylimi's court, a messenger came from King Lygni to ask the hand of Hiordis. Lygni's kingdom was near Eylimi's, and Sigmund's was far away. Lygni was young, and Sigmund was old. Both were rich and powerful kings.

Eylimi listened to both messages, but had no word to say. He asked both earls to wait, and while they were entertained in the banquet hall, he sought his daughter and told her of her suitors. She chose the Völsung king.

The old king went out with a sad heart, for he thought that the young king Lygni would make a more suitable husband for Hiordis. But he had said that she should have her way, and he could not change her choice. So he sent rich gifts to Lygni, with the word that his daughter was betrothed to another king; and King Sigmund's earl received the welcome news, that in two months' time his royal master might come for his bride. 'But', said Eylimi, 'bid him come with sword and ships of war, for I fear that he may be attacked.'

But Sigmund remembered his father, and scorned to take an army to a wedding. Still he prepared ten long ships, and filled them with the best of his men. They arrived at Eylimi's kingdom without accident, and received a warm welcome.

White-haired Sigmund and fair Hiordis were greatly pleased

with each other, and the wedding feasts were joyful. Eylimi loved Sigmund for his goodness, and admired him for his wisdom and dignity. He no longer feared for the happiness of Hiordis because she had chosen an old king for her husband. But one day, sails were seen approaching the island. Lygni was angry at the refusal of Hiordis, and said that he would have the princess as well as the gifts. He came, with a fleet and army, on the day that Sigmund and Hiordis had intended to sail for the land of the Völsungs.

Sorrow and dread filled the heart of Eylimi; but Sigmund bade him be of good cheer, for he said that, even if he had not come, Hiordis could never have been persuaded to marry Lygni. He cut the peace strings from his sword, and set his little army in battle array.

It is said that the number of Sigmund's and Eylimi's men was to the hosts of Lygni as the brown pips are to an apple when it is cut through the core. But the little army marched out bravely, and Hiordis, with her maid, followed at a distance.

Sigmund stood like an image of gold, in the front of the battle, with the sword of the Branstock unsheathed. As the hosts of Lygni advanced, it seemed as if the whole world were moving. But the flashing sword of Odin hewed down all that came within its reach, as Sigmund wielded it with more than youthful vigour. He was no longer worn and old; the hope and eagerness of youth had come back in the excitement of the battle, and he said to himself, 'A few more strokes of the sword, and I shall have conquered the world.'

But an old, one-eyed man, wearing a broad-brimmed hat and a cloud-grey cloak, made his way across the battlefield. He carried a heavy spear, with which he struck the sword of the Branstock, and the sword fell in pieces at Sigmund's feet. The old man vanished; and the advancing army of Lygni struck down Sigmund. His warriors fell like grass before the scythe, and the only ones left standing were Lygni's men.

'Who will now oppose King Lygni's wooing?' cried the king; and he led the way to Eylimi's palace.

When the last warrior had left the battlefield, Hiordis came out from the thicket, to look for her husband. She found him wounded, but still alive. He opened his eyes as she bent over him, and she cried out with delight. But he said: 'I cannot live; this day my eyes have seen Odin, and I must do his will. Take the pieces of my sword, the sword of the Branstock, and keep them as your choicest treasure. If the gods give you a son, he will be a greater hero than the Völsung race has yet known. Give the broken sword to him when he has grown to manhood, and the new-welded blade will be invincible. Put away your sorrow, for, even now, I see the light, and hear the music, in the great banquet hall of Odin's heroes.'

V. THE BURIAL OF SIGMUND

Hiordis lingered beside her dead until day began to dawn. As she looked toward the sea, she saw a warship approaching the shore. She returned to the thicket, where her maid was waiting, and told her of the death of Sigmund, and of the ship that she had seen. 'Now,' she said, 'give me your dress of blue, and take my purple and gold. And, when the men ask our names, say that you are Hiordis, the wife of King Völsung, and that I am your handmaid.'

When the ship's company landed, they were led by a king, Elf, the son of the Helper. He had just come from war, and had turned his ship toward the island, in the hope of finding water. As they drew near the shore, they saw that there had been a great battle; and they noticed that a woman, dressed like a queen and wearing a gold crown, sat among the slain. She ran into a thicket; and they lost sight of her.

They went directly to the battlefield, and at once recognized the body of Sigmund as that of a great king. 'Come,' said King Elf, 'and look upon his face. Few such are left on earth. Then let us go to the thicket, where the queen is hidden; and learn from her the story of the mighty dead.'

They found the women, and greeted them kindly. To their questions, the one in the queen's dress answered: 'I am Hiordis, the queen. The slain lord in yonder field was my husband, Sigmund, the Völsung.'

'And who is this blue-clad one?' asked King Elf. 'She is my waiting maid, who weeps for her lover, killed in the battle,' answered the queen.

The king looked again at the maid's sorrowful face, but said no more. He went, with the women, to the battlefield, and built a mound for Sigmund, the Völsung. The walls were made of the broken shields of his foes, and hung with their banners. His sword could not be found; and the maid explained that her royal master had commanded that the pieces of his broken sword be taken by the queen.

After Sigmund's body had been laid in the mound, King Elf asked the women where they would go, since the island was in the hands of Lygni. Hiordis asked that they might go, with him, to his home. The king gladly gave them passage in his warship; and they sailed to the happy land of King Elf and his father, the Helper.

THE HOUSE OF THE HELPER

as told by Sarah Powers Bradish

I. KING ELF FINDS OUT THE QUEEN

The Helper and his wife gave their unexpected guests a cordial welcome; and Hiordis was comforted by the kindness of her new friends.

One morning Elf's mother said to her son, 'I have observed these women carefully, and I should like to know why the inferior woman is the better dressed.'

Elf said, 'She is Hiordis, wife of Sigmund, the Völsung.'

The old queen laughed aloud, and said: 'It is not so, my son. Have you not noticed that the handmaid speaks whenever any matter of importance is to be decided?'

'Yes,' he said, 'and she is both wise and gracious, and very dear to me.'

'Follow my advice,' said the wise queen mother, 'and, when you have won your queen, see if they do not again change raiment.'

One day Elf said to the woman in purple and gold, 'How do you know, in the dark winter mornings, when it is time to rise?'

She answered: 'When I lived in my father's house, the folks must be astir, whether the fields were light or dark. I rose early to go to the meadows, and drank milk before I left the house; and now I am always thirsty when it is time to rise.'

Elf laughed, and said: 'That was a strange custom that required a king's daughter to go to the fields before light. And now, fair maid with eyes of grey, how can you tell that morning has come, when the heavens are as dark as midnight?'

She said: 'My father gave me this gold ring, which has this strange property: it grows cold upon my finger when day comes. So when my ring grows cold, I know it is time to rise.'

Elf laughed again. 'Indeed,' he said, 'there was gold in your father's house. Come now, tell me that you are Hiordis, wife of Sigmund, the Völsung; and I will make you queen of my people.'

'Give me a year to mourn for Sigmund, and then I will be your queen,' she said.

II. THE BIRTH OF SIGURD, THE VÖLSUNG

There was peace in the land of the Helper, and joy in King Elf's home, for a beautiful babe lay in the arms of Hiordis. His eyes were so bright that the women shrank from their gaze, and so strong that they could look at the sun. Hiordis held him close, while she told him the story of Sigmund, and then gave him to the women to show to the kings.

The Helper and his son were sitting on their high-seat, when they heard the sound of music, and four women, dressed in white, entered the hall.

'O daughters of earls,' said the Helper, 'what tidings do you bring?'

The women talked of grief, wonder, fear and joy, until King Elf grew impatient and cried out, 'Yet you come rejoicing; what have you to tell?' Then they advanced to the high-seat; and, drawing away the purple covering, presented the child, and said, 'Queen

Hiordis sends you this; and she says that he shall be called by the name that you shall give him.'

King Elf took the child in his arms, and held him a long time, while he thought of all that Hiordis had told him, of the might of the Völsungs, and the battle by the sea. Then he said, 'His name shall be Sigurd, the Völsung,' and sprinkled water upon the head of the young prince.

Men heard the name, and echoed it through hall and courtyard and market place. Hiordis heard it in her chamber; and, when the women returned with the baby, before they could speak, she greeted him as Sigurd, the Völsung.

Sigurd grew in beauty and wisdom; and, after a time, his mother Hiordis was married to King Elf. Peace and plenty blessed the land.

III. GREYFELL

Two ancient men lived in the country of the Helper. One was related to the giants, and the other to the dwarfs. Gripir was tall and stately, with hair and beard of snowy white. He knew all things, from the beginning of the world; and he knew many things that were to be.

Regin was beardless, crooked and short. His face was pinched and wan. He was so old that no one knew how long he had lived in the land of the Helper. He was skilled in everything except the arts of war. He was eloquent, and men believed every word he spoke. He sang and played the harp most beautifully. He could read the clouds and the winds, and still the sea. He could bind up wounds, and heal the sick. He taught men how to sow and reap;

how to spin and weave. He was master of all work in metals. He loved young Sigurd, and asked to be his teacher.

The Helper said: 'You taught me, and you taught my son. We know you are the master of masters. Three times man's lifetime would not be long enough to learn your wisdom. Yet your heart is cold. We love young Sigurd, and would not have you make him grim and ill-tempered.'

Regin laughed as he answered, 'I taught you cunning by measure; but I shall measure nothing to him; I shall not make him cold-hearted or ill-natured.'

So Regin took Sigurd to his house in the forest, where he taught the young prince all things, except the art of war. He taught him to make swords, and all kinds of weapons and armour. He also taught him many languages, how to carve runes, and how to play the harp and to sing. He taught him the haunts of wild animals, the names and uses of flowers and plants; how to ply the oar and spread the sails on the sea.

One day, as they sat by the forge, Regin told tales of ancient kings and heroes, until Sigurd's heart swelled within him, and his longing to do noble things gave a new light to his eyes.

Regin said, 'You will go out into the world, to do greater and braver deeds than your fathers ever did.'

But the boy shook his head, and said, 'I love the Helper and King Elf; their land is fair and good.'

'Yet do as I bid you,' said Regin. 'Ask for a war horse.'

The lad was angry, as he replied: 'I have all the horses I need, and everything I want. Why would you have me ask for more?'

'The Völsungs were a noble race,' said Regin. 'They were not satisfied with good, but demanded the best.' Then he took his harp, and sang of the deeds of the heroes and of the rides of the Valkyries, until Sigurd forgot his anger. He left the forge, with the song ringing in his ears; and that night he asked the kings to give him such a horse as he might choose.

'The stables are open to you,' answered King Elf.

But Sigurd begged a token for Gripir, who had charge of all the horses; so that he might take the best of the strong and the swift. 'But,' he added, 'if I ask too great a gift, I pray you, forget what I have said.'

King Elf smiled, and said: 'You will take a long ride. You will see war and sorrow, and death at last; but you will win praise and honour. So have your way, for we can no more hold you than we can hold back the rising sun.'

Sigurd thanked the kings; and, early next morning, went to Gripir. The wise old man lived in a house on a mountain crag. Eagles flew about it; and winds from the heart of the mountains blew through every room. Few men dared step across the threshold. Sigurd entered the hall, and found Gripir seated in a chair made from a sea serpent's tooth. His beard almost swept the sea-green floor. His robe was made of gold, and his staff had a knob of crystal.

Gripir knew Sigurd, and said: 'Hail, king with the bright eyes! You need no token, nor need you tell your errand. The wind brought me word that you were coming to choose a war horse from my meadows. Now go, and take the best; but come back when you have your sword.'

Sigurd ran down the mountain side, and was on his way to the meadows, when he met a man wearing a broad-brimmed hat, and a cloud-grey cloak. He had but one eye, and he seemed very old. He spoke to Sigurd, and said, 'Let me tell you how to choose your horse.'

'Are you Gripir's horseherd?' asked Sigurd; and he had begun to ask the old man whether he would take gold for his advice, when he noticed his noble bearing, and said, 'Your face is like that of the heroes, my master, Regin, tells me about; and your cloud-grey garment I have seen in my dreams.'

'There is one horse in the meadow, better than all the rest,' said the stranger; 'and if you would have him for your own, follow my directions.'

Sigurd said, 'What shall I do?'

'Drive all the horses into the river,' said the old man; 'and wait, to see what happens.'

Sigurd drove them into the water; but the current was so strong that it carried many fine horses out to sea. Some turned and swam back to the bank; others were caught in the eddies and drowned. But one swam across the river, climbed the opposite bank, and galloped over the meadows on the other side. Then he wheeled, leaped into the river, and swam back. He shook the water from his mane, and stood neighing at Sigurd's side.

'Listen, Sigurd,' said the old man. 'I gave your father a gift which you will yet hold dear; and I now give you this horse. Do not fear to go where he may carry you, for your fathers are now in my house, enjoying the rewards of their valour. Like all your noble race, live so that you will not care when death may come.'

Then Sigurd knew that Odin had come to him, and would have asked about many things, but Odin faded away, and only Greyfell stood beside his master on the river bank.

REGIN'S STORY

as told by Sarah Powers Bradish

I. REIDMAR AND HIS SONS

One day when Sigurd was sitting with Regin, the dwarf told stories of kings who had won their crowns by many hard-fought battles. At last he said: 'You are Sigmund's son; will you wait till these peaceful kings of this little kingdom are dead, and then will you serve their sons? Will you spend your life in idle waiting for the time when their war banners shall float in the breeze?'

Sigurd answered: 'You taunt me too much. I love these peaceful kings; their land is good. Perhaps the time may come when I shall be called to do some daring deed. When the call is heard, and the deed is ready, the man will not be wanting.'

Regin replied: 'The deed is ready, but you love this land, and why should he who can feast be content to eat rye bread? They say that you are Sigmund's son, but you need not be a warrior, for Sigmund lies quiet in his mound by the sea.'

Sigurd's eyes flashed as he said, 'Mock not the son of Sigmund, but tell the deed that waits.'

The cunning master answered, 'The deed is the righting of wrong, and the winning of great treasure.'

Sigurd asked: 'How long have you known of this? And what is the treasure to you?'

'I have known of the wrong,' said Regin, 'for hundreds of years. And the treasure is mine, but it is beyond my reach; for I know nothing of the art of war. I came to this land to seek a hero to undo the wrong, and bring back my treasure; but generations passed, and the end seemed no nearer, until I saw your eyes in the cradle.'

Sigurd was silent, but at last he said: 'I will do the deed, and you shall have your treasure, and the curse also (if a curse rests upon the gold); but I will surely do the deed. Tell me where the treasure lies.'

Regin answered, 'I must first tell you the story of my life; so keep your seat and listen to a tale of things that happened before kings were born.

'I belong to the race of the dwarfs. We knew no right nor wrong; we had no love; we made and unmade, and felt no sorrow. We were wise and powerful, and our day is not wholly past. Trust not your life in my hands when I dream of my kindred, and when I seem most like the dwarfs of long ago.

'After a time the gods came among us, and we learned to love, and hope, and fear. We lived in the depths of the earth, and learned to work in metals. We knew of poisons and medicines; we made the spear and bow; we built ships to sail on the sea.

'Reidmar was my father. He was old and wise. To my brother, Fafnir, he gave a soul that knew no fear, a brow like hardened iron, a hand that never failed, an ear that could not listen to a sorrowful tale and a heart as greedy as a king's. To my brother, Otter, he gave a snare and a longing to search the forests and streams until nothing was left alive. To me, the youngest, he gave memory of the past, fear of the future, a hammer, an anvil and coals of fire burning in the forge.

'Now we were but little better than men; but we still had the power to change our shape, and appear in whatever form we would. Fafnir went abroad and became the terror of the world. Otter lived with the animals that he hunted, and so often took their forms that he seemed to be the king of the forest. I toiled to build my father's house, and, as the walls rose bright with gold, my hands became soiled and misshapen, and I looked upon the sun and the wind and all things in nature as only the tools of my smithy.

II. THE THREE TRAVELLERS

After a time, three travellers came from Asgard to look over their work. They were Odin, Hoenir and Loki. They passed through a forest and came to a river where they found an otter eating a fish. Loki picked up a stone and threw it at the otter, which fell dead. Loki took both the otter and the fish and went on with his companions. They soon came to a house at the foot of a mountain. They were tired and hungry, and, as the sun was setting, Odin said to his brothers, 'Let us seek shelter for the night in this house.'

'They found the master of the house seated in a golden hall, on a chair made from a whale's tooth. His robe was purple, and he wore a crown of gold.

'He had no sword, and received his guests kindly. He ordered a feast spread before them; and sweet music played while they ate. But, in the midst of the feast, they felt they were under a spell, so they could not throw off the semblance of men. Besides, they were unarmed, and Odin had foolishly lent his spear, Gungnir. Their host taunted them with their helplessness.

'Loki had thrown down the dead otter when he entered the hall. Fafnir and I recognized our brother Otter; and we knew that our father, Reidmar, would demand satisfaction for his death. When his guests were completely under his control, Reidmar told them that they had killed his son, Otter, and that they were his prisoners until they could atone for the offence.

'Then Odin said: 'We have indeed done you a grievous wrong; but we will do what we can to compensate you for the injury. You love gold; we will give you gold. It is for you to say how much.'

'Then Reidmar, Fafnir and I cried out with one voice, 'You shall die, and we will rule the world.'

'Odin answered with calm and awful voice, 'Be just, O Reidmar! How much gold do you require?'

'Then covetous Reidmar forgot his anger and his wisdom; his greed alone spoke out, 'Give me the Flame of the Waters and the Gold of the Sea, which Andvari hides beneath a mountain, until every hair of this dead otter is covered.'

''Let Loki fetch it,' said Odin; and I released the mischief maker from his bonds.

'In the most distant part of the world there is a place called the Desert of Dread. A great river falls over a terrible precipice; and that waterfall is called the force of Andvari. Andvari was a dark elf who lived alone in the land of cloudy waste. Long years ago, he knew of the sun and stars, the sea and land; but he forgot them all in his love of gold. He knew nothing of men or gods; he heeded neither cold nor heat; he knew not night from day; he had forgotten even his name. He took no rest, but toiled constantly, always gathering gold, gold, nothing but gold.

'Loki found the desert and the waterfall, but he saw nothing of the elf. At last he remembered that Andvari took the gold from the water. So he went to the river; and, looking down into the water, saw a salmon, which he thought must be Andvari, who had taken fright at the sound of footsteps. The salmon was too wary to be taken with a hook; so Loki went to borrow a net from Ran, who, at that time, had the only net in the world. She was very careful of it; but after much trouble, Loki induced her to lend it to him, to catch the owner of the Flame of the Sea.

'Loki stretched the net across the river, and took Andvari in its meshes. When the elf felt the tightening of the cords, he remembered gods and men and his own name; and when Loki lifted him from the water, he took his own form, and said, 'You know that I am Andvari, and you have come to take my gold.'

'He led Loki into his storehouse and gave him all his gold, even the hauberk of gold, and the Helmet of Dread. When the last piece had been delivered, Andvari turned away, and Loki saw something glitter on his finger, which he made the elf give to him.

'As Andvari drew the ring from his finger, he said: 'I can spare all the rest better than this; for this is the seed of the gold; and with it I can make more gold. But take that, if you will. My curse shall go with it; and, to whomever it is given, he shall have the curse.'

'Loki placed the ring on his finger, and brought the gold to my father's house. When all that golden treasure was heaped upon our floor, it seemed as if the sun itself were shining within our walls.

'Then Odin said to Reidmar, 'The ransom is paid.' But Reidmar said, 'We do not know whether the gold will cover the body of the otter.' So Fafnir and I brought in the otter, and piled the gold around it, until it was all covered, as we thought; but we had taken every piece of the gold. Then Reidmar caught the gleam of the ring, and, at the same time, discovered a hair near the otter's mouth; and he said, 'You shall be my slaves till you give me that ring, the seed of gold and grief, to cover this one hair.'

'Then Odin took the ring from Loki's finger and threw it upon the heap, saying, 'I am glad you have it all, even the curse of the elf king.'

'Reidmar laughed, as he answered: 'Who shall do me harm? My sword is Fafnir, and my shield is Regin, the smith.'

'I struck the shackles from the gods, and they went out into the night; but, at the door, Odin turned and warned us of the danger of the love of gold. Then they went away; and the gold was ours.

III. THE CURSE OF THE RING

I looked upon the gold, and loved it, as it shone upon our faces like the sun. I longed for it, but smiled and begged my father to keep the greater part, but to give Fafnir a share, and me a little handful, for my skill as a smith, and for my help that day. But I might have asked for much or little; for he made no answer. He sat on his ivory throne, and stared at the gold. Fafnir did not speak, but looked at the gold and our father.

'We watched the gold till morning; when Fafnir took his sword, and I, my hammer; and we went out into the world. I came back at night; and, while I longed to see the gold, I dared not go into the hall where it lay. As I lay in my bed, I thought I heard the clink of the gold, and saw the light. I slept, and dreamed, and woke with a cry. I sprang from my bed, and ran to the hall. Fafnir stood by the gold: at his feet lay our father, whose body was covered with gold, and whose face became white, in death, as I looked. Fafnir wore the Helmet of Dread; and he held his bare sword in his hand.

''I shall keep the gold,' he said, 'and shall live alone, to guard the gold and take its curse. Will you leave me, or stay until I shed your blood?'

'I fled from the house with neither gold nor tools. I had only my remembering heart and my skilful hands. I came to this land, and taught men to sow and reap; and men said that Freyr had taught them husbandry.

'I taught them to work in metals, to sail on the sea, and to tame and use horses; and they said that Thor had taught them all these things. I gave the shuttle to maidens, and taught them to weave; and the needle, and taught them to sew; and, when they were old, they said that they had learned these things from Freyja.

'I taught them poetry and music; and they said that Bragi was their teacher, while I was a wandering skald. Still I became a master of masters. But I shall meet my fate by a sword in the hand of a stripling.

'I became wise; but I longed for my brother's gold; and I envied him, when kings gave me golden gifts to pay for my skill. Once I went back to my native land, and found the fields lying wasted and desolate. The house was falling; the roof was gone. I looked into the hall, and saw the gold and a great dragon coiled about it. I fled again; and, many years after, I heard men tell of the treasure of gold, that lay on the Glittering Heath, guarded by a dreadful serpent.

'Then I knew the Völsung race; and, at last, I saw you in the house of the Helper. I dreamed dreams, saw your glory, and knew that your sword would win my treasure.

'I think that Fafnir was wiser than I, because he did not waste his treasure on men. But I shall have it all, some day; and then I shall be king of men.'

Then he slept, and Sigurd rose, and cried 'Awake, O master.'

Regin opened his eyes, and said: 'Have you listened, Sigurd? Will you avenge the wrong, and win the treasure?'

And Sigurd, looking at him with clear eyes, said, 'You shall have the treasure and the curse.'

THE FORGING OF THE SWORD

as told by Sarah Powers Bradish

I. REGIN'S FAILURES

Sigurd came to Regin again, and said, 'I ask a gift at your hands.'

Regin answered, 'I would reach to the end of the world, to find the gift you need.'

'But the gift I require lies near you,' said Sigurd; 'I want you to forge me a sword.'

'Here is your sword,' said Regin, 'wrought with many charms. I began it when the waning moon was new.'

Sigurd took the sword, and looked at the jewelled hilt, and the runes engraved upon the blade, while Regin waited for a word of approval. Sigurd turned and struck the anvil with it; the sword fell in pieces on the earth. Then he went out into the forest.

When two moons had waxed and waned, Sigurd came again to ask about his sword; and Regin said, 'I have worked day and night, and my hand has surely lost its cunning, if this fails to satisfy you.'

Sigurd struck with it the anvil again; and again the pieces of the sword were shattered.

The next day Sigurd said to his mother, 'Where are the pieces of the sword of the Branstock, mother?'

'Are you angry, my son?' she asked.

'No, mother; but the time for deeds has come.'

She took his hand, and led him to her treasure chamber; and, unrolling bands of silk, showed him the pieces of his father's sword, which gleamed as white as silver; and the jewels in the hilt shone with as bright a light as when Sigmund plucked it from the oak.

Sigurd smiled, and said: 'You have kept your charge well; but your watch is over now. These pieces shall be welded to shine again in the rain of Odin.'

She gave him the sacred steel that she had guarded so faithfully. He kissed her gently, and left her standing alone. She did not speak; but, with eager eyes, she watched her godlike son, who had grown so tall and fair and glorious.

II. THE WRATH OF SIGURD

Sigurd went swiftly to Regin's smithy, and gave him the pieces of the broken sword.

'Will nothing else satisfy you?' asked Regin. 'This sword, that I fashioned long ago, brought death to your father's father, and to all his sons.'

'With this sword I shall slay the serpent and win the gold,' said Sigurd. 'It is too late to turn back from the path you bade me take.'

When the moon of May was full, Sigurd again sought Regin at midnight. The dwarf was worn and pale, but he said, 'I have done as you wished,' and gave Sigurd the welded sword.

Sigurd raised it high above his head, as his father raised it, when he drew it from the Branstock. Then, as he struck a fearful blow upon the anvil, he shouted for joy; for he held the sword, unhurt in his hand, while the anvil was cut in two.

Then Regin took his harp, and sang about making the sword, which he called the Wrath of Sigurd. He sang of how he had forged it long ago, and how he had welded and wrought it again.

Sigurd listened to the song, and said: 'I will avenge your wrong, for you have failed me in nothing. The sword is all I could ask.'

'Come,' said Regin, 'let us try the sword in another way.'

They went out to the river, and Regin threw a lock of wool into the stream, and held the sword in the water until the current brought it against the blade, which cut the wool in two.

Then they placed the Wrath of Sigurd in a golden sheath, and tied the peace strings.

THE PROPHECY OF GRIPIR

as told by Sarah Powers Bradish

The next morning Sigurd mounted Greyfell, and rode again to Gripir's house. He entered the hall, and stood leaning on his sword, while he saluted the ancient king.

Gripir said, 'Hail, Sigurd!' and welcomed him to his home.

Sigurd said: 'Hail, father! I have my new sword, and have come for your parting word.'

'What would you hear?' asked Gripir.

'Your word and the Norns'.'

'What sight would you see?'

'I would see as the gods see; though the sight be dreadful.'

'What hope would you hope?'

'Your hope and the gods'.'

The ancient king was silent as he looked at Sigurd, and thought of the future of the youth. Then he spoke of that future, and told Sigurd that he would do valiant deeds, win great wealth, and live with the Cloudy People; but his glorious day would be short.

Then he called Sigurd to sit beside him on his throne, and told him of mighty deeds, of distant lands, of the sea and heavens.

Then Sigurd said that he must not linger, for a war horse as swift as the wind, and his father's sword, had been given him; that he must obey the voice that called him to ride to the Glittering Heath.

So the old king bade the young warrior farewell, and Sigurd returned to Regin when the sun was sinking in the west.

THE GLITTERING HEATH

as told by Sarah Powers Bradish

I. ODIN DIRECTS SIGURD

The next morning Sigurd rode away with Regin for guide. They soon left the pleasant land of the Helper, and came to the hill country. All day they climbed higher and higher, and at night they slept upon a mountain top. In the morning they looked back to the beautiful country where Sigurd had spent his boyhood, and forward to the range of mountains that rose like a wall before them. For three days they rode over mountains and across deserts. The fourth day they came to a desolate region that was as brass under Greyfell's hoofs. This was the entrance to the Glittering Heath. Sigurd dismounted, and walked carefully in the thick fog to meet the terrible dragon.

Regin had fallen back, but Sigurd hardly missed him, he was so intent on finding the guardian of the treasure. Suddenly a man appeared in his path, one-eyed and old, wrapped in a cloud-grey cloak, and wearing a broad-brimmed hat.

'Hail, Sigurd!' he said.

'Hail! I greet you, my friend and my father's friend,' answered Sigurd.

Odin asked where Sigurd was going. Sigurd answered that he was going to slay the dragon that guarded the golden treasure.

'Then let me tell you what to do,' said Odin. 'You will find a slot worn in the stone. It is the path worn by the dragon in his daily journey after water. Dig a pit in this path, and lie in it with your naked sword in your hand.'

Sigurd worked all night; and at daybreak the pit was dug. He lay in it, with his sword in his hand. The light was growing brighter, when he heard a noise like the trampling of many feet, and the tinkle and clatter of gold dragged over the earth. The sounds came nearer, and the light was shut off. It seemed to Sigurd that an inky river rolled over the pit, and the air was heavy with the poisonous breath of the serpent; when Sigurd made an upward thrust with his sword, and pierced the heart of the dragon. Then he leaped out; and, as he stood with uplifted sword by the side of the dead monster, seven eagles settled on a mountain peak, and uttered hoarse cries.

Sigurd was still standing by the dragon, when Regin came up and reproached him with the murder of his brother.

'I have done your deed,' said Sigurd; 'and now we must part.'

'You have slain my brother,' said Regin; 'what atonement can you make?'

'Take the gold,' said Sigurd, 'as a ransom for my head.'

'You have slain my brother,' repeated Regin. Then he drew his sword, and cut a piece of the dragon's flesh, which he ordered Sigurd to cook for him, while he lay down and slept.

Sigurd found waste wood in the heath, with which he made a fire. He fixed the piece of flesh on a spit, and held it to roast. The eagles flew down, and sat near him, while he cooked. He put out his hand, to see whether the meat were done; and some of the juice of the dripping meat fell on it, and burned his finger. He unconsciously put his finger into his mouth, and tasted the meat juice. Then he understood what the eagles were saying.

II. THE EAGLES' COUNSEL

The first eagle asked why he waited so long to roast the meat. The second said, 'Go, for the king's feast awaits you.'

The third said, 'How great is the feast of him who feeds on wisdom.'

The fourth said, 'Will you let Regin live, to spread waste and ruin over the world?'

The fifth said, 'Regin knew that a youth would slay him; but he intends to slay the youth.'

The sixth said, 'He has lost all sense of truth, in his greed for gold.'

The seventh said, 'Hasten, Sigurd! Strike while he dreams.'

Then Sigurd, for the second time, lifted his sword; and Regin lay dead beside the dragon, slain by the stripling for whom he had forged the sword, and whom he had planned to kill.

III. SIGURD TAKES THE TREASURE AND THE CURSE

Sigurd sheathed his sword, and mounted Greyfell. The eagles flew about his head, as he rode along the path of the serpent, to the ruins of the golden house, of which Regin had told him. The hoard of gold lay in heaps upon the floor. There were coins from ancient cities, golden armour, magic rings and bracelets, and blocks of gold, just as the elfin miners had cut them from the rock. The hauberk of gold and the Helmet of Dread lay with the rest. Brighter than all gleamed Andvari's ring; the ring that Loki had taken, that Odin had asked for, and that Reidmar had demanded to cover the last hair of the otter; the ring that bore the curse.

Sigurd put on the hauberk of gold, the Helmet of Dread, and the fatal ring. Then he carried out the gold, while the eagles screamed, 'Bind the red rings, O Sigurd.'

He worked all night; and, in the morning, took Greyfell by the bridle, to lead him from the Glittering Heath, because he thought that the weight of the gold was enough for the horse to carry. But Greyfell refused to stir, until Sigurd, clad in all his armour, vaulted into the saddle; when he bore his royal master across the desolate waste, to the green world beyond.

BRYNHILD

as told by Sarah Powers Bradish

I. THE SLEEPING MAIDEN

Day after day, Sigurd rode, always rising higher and higher, until he came to a lofty mountain. Its peak was capped with clouds, through which fire seemed ready to burst. Sigurd thought that, from the top of this mountain, he could get a view of the country he was about to cross; so he began the ascent. The fire burned brighter and brighter, until flames appeared above the clouds. Then the clouds thickened, and hid the mountain. Night fell around them; but Sigurd encouraged Greyfell; and they went on in the darkness.

As they climbed up a great rock, the whole summit appeared as a mass of flame. At dawn they came to a plain, from which they could see the topmost peak, surrounded by a circle of fire. But neither horse nor rider hesitated.

As they approached the flaming wall, Sigurd bent low over the horse's neck, and spoke kindly to him. Then he tightened the saddle girth, grasped the reins firmly, and, with his sword unsheathed in his right hand, urged Greyfell to make the daring leap.

Greyfell plunged into the flames, which had blazed more fiercely as horse and rider approached the circle. As they dashed through it, the fire leaped up as if to grasp them both, and then died away, leaving a ring of white ashes.

A castle stood before them. Sigurd entered the open gate and passed through the hall. He came to a mound, on which lay a warrior clad in armour. Sigurd unclasped the warrior's helmet, and beheld the face of a sleeping woman. He cut the rings of her armour with his sword; and she still lay asleep, dressed in fine white linen, with her golden hair covering her breast. Sigurd knelt beside her and woke her with a kiss.

II. THE MAIDEN TELLS HER NAME

'What is your name, O fairest of the earth?' he said. 'I am Sigurd, son of Völsung. I have slain the terrible dragon and taken the hoard of gold.'

She answered: 'My name is Brynhild. I was one of the daughters of earth, but the All-Father took me, and made me a Shield maiden. I was one of the band of Valkyries, who hovered over battlefields, to decide victories, and to bear the slain to Odin's halls. Once he sent me to attend a single combat, and bade me give the victory to an ancient robber king. I knew the story of the quarrel which led to this fight; and I loved the fair maiden who must wed the victor. So I pricked the robber with the point of my sword, and carried him to Valhalla; and left the handsome young lover to take his bride.

'For my disobedience, Odin said that I must again become a woman, and also a wife. I begged that my husband might be a hero, who knew no fear. Odin said, 'That request I will grant, but you will have long to wait for that hero.'

'He brought me to the top of this mountain, Hindfell, and pricked me with a sleep thorn; and, striking the rocks with his spear, made the ring of flickering flame, through which you rode. I knew no more until you woke me just now.'

Then she talked with Sigurd; and her words showed that she was the wisest as well as the most beautiful of women.

III. THE BETROTHAL

Brynhild was satisfied that Sigurd was a fearless hero; so it was settled that they should be married at her sister's home in Lymdale, where she would go at once.

Sigurd said:

> 'O Brynhild, now hearken while I swear,
> That the sun shall die in the heavens, and the day no more be fair,
> If I seek not love in Lymdale, and the house that fostered thee.
> And the land where thou awakest 'twixt the woodland and the sea!'

Brynhild answered:

> 'O Sigurd, Sigurd, now hearken while I swear,
> That the day shall die forever, and the sun to blackness wear.
> Ere I forget thee, Sigurd, as I lie 'twixt wood and sea,

In the little land of Lymdale, and the house that fostered
   me.'

Then Sigurd, forgetting the curse, placed on her finger the ring of Andvari. After this he remounted Greyfell and rode onward over the mountain. But Brynhild hastened to the house of her sister in Lymdale.

GUDRUN'S DREAMS

as told by Sarah Powers Bradish

I. WHY THE PRINCESS WAS SAD

In the Land of Cloudy Mists lived a people known as the Niblungs. They were brave and warlike, and had never known defeat in battle. Their king and queen were Giuki and Grimhild, who had three sons and one daughter. The eldest son, Gunnar, was tall and fair; the second, Hogni, was very wise; the third, Guttorm, was a great warrior; and their daughter, Gudrun, was very beautiful.

One morning Gudrun, who was as charming in manner as she was pleasing in person, passed down the garden walk, without speaking to any of her attendants. Her nurse came to ask her why she had left unnoticed the things of which she was so fond; why she did not speak to her maidens, or go to her embroidery, or join in the chase.

'Tomorrow I shall do as I have always done,' she answered; 'today I am sad, because I cannot forget the dream that came to me last night.'

'Tell me your dream,' said the nurse; 'for dreams often indicate only the weather.'

Gudrun said: 'I thought I sat by the door of my father's hall, and saw a falcon come from the north. His feathers were golden, and his eyes were as bright as crystal in the sunshine. Men feared him, but I felt no fear. My heart was light with hope. He hovered over the Niblung palace, and then flew down to my knees. He cried out to me, and I clasped him in my arms.'

'This falcon is a king's son,' said the nurse, 'who has won honour for his noble deeds, and will come to ask you to be his bride.'

'You give good interpretations to my dreams, because you love me,' said Gudrun. 'My mother, Grimhild, is also wise; but she turns my dreams to evil.'

'Your dream is easy to read, and its meaning is good,' said the nurse; 'but, if you are in doubt, let us go to Lymdale, to consult Brynhild, who is skilful in all such matters. She will give the same meaning that I have given; but your confidence in her will give you peace.'

'Let us go to Brynhild,' said Gudrun.

II. THE VISIT TO BRYNHILD

So the wagons were prepared, the maidens dressed for travel, and Gudrun hastened to Lymdale. When they arrived at the white castle by the sea, Brynhild's maidens came out to meet them, and lead them into the hall. Brynhild had been sitting at her embroidery, and she led Gudrun to the frames, on which she was working pictures of great deeds. For a while, they asked and answered questions about each other's friends; then the maidens brought a dainty repast, and talked of kings and heroes, and asked who was the greatest hero. Brynhild spoke of kings of distant lands, and Gudrun said, 'Why do you not name my brothers, who are called the greatest men of our time?'

'Your brothers are great kings,' answered Brynhild, 'but I have seen one greater than they. His name is Sigurd the Völsung, son of King Sigmund.'

Gudrun trembled and turned pale, but asked, 'How do you know that Sigurd is the greatest king?'

'His mother went to the battlefield,' said Brynhild, 'and found King Sigmund lying among the slain. He was mortally wounded, but still alive. He told her that her son would be a greater king than he, and he had been greater than any king who ever lived.

'Young Sigurd was brought up in the house of the Helper, and every day he did some wonderful thing. He has already killed the terrible dragon that guarded the golden treasure, and he will soon come to us across the mountains.'

Gudrun was silent, then rose and said: 'It is late; the guard of the Niblung gate looks in vain for the light dust of our golden wagons. Come with your maidens to my father's house, and we will welcome you, as you have welcomed us today.'

Brynhild thanked her for her kind and cheerful words, but looked into her sad eyes, and said, 'Stay with your friends, who wish you only happiness.'

Then Gudrun said: 'I came to tell you my dreams, for I knew you were wise and true. I dare not tell my mother, and I fear the mocking laughter of the wise women, when they hear a maiden's dream.'

'I shall not mock,' said Brynhild, 'but I may not be able to give you the help you need.'

'This was my dream,' said Gudrun: 'I thought I was sitting at the door one morning, when a falcon came out of the north. He flew over the kingdoms of men, and filled their hearts with fear. Then he circled about the Niblung castle, and my heart beat high with hope. He was a beautiful creature; his feathers were like gold, and his eyes flashed like crystal in the sunshine. He flew down to my knees, and I took him in my arms.'

'That is indeed a good dream,' said Brynhild. 'A great king will make you his queen.'

'I have not told you all,' said Gudrun. 'With joy I clasped him to my breast, and it was stained with purple blood. My heart grew cold and heavy as lead. I laid my hand upon it, and my falcon was gone.'

Now Brynhild was pale, but she said: 'Fear not, O daughter of Niblungs. The king will come and wed you, and you will be happy. Do not think it strange that changes should come to a great and warlike race. Your husband will fall dead beside you, but that is not the worst that could befall you. Do not think of his death, but of his glorious career.'

'After this dream, I dreamed again,' said Gudrun. 'I thought I sat in the garden, and a hart came out of the forest. His hair was golden, and his antlers glittered in the sun. He was the noblest deer ever seen. He came to me and laid his head upon my arm. Then a fair queen came and sat beside me. The heavens grew black, and in the gathering darkness I saw a hand and arm, with the jewels and rings of the queen. There was a sudden sword thrust, and my beautiful hart lay dead at my feet.

'I cried out in anguish. I was no longer in the garden, but in the depths of the forest. Wild wolves howled around me, and I called them my friends. I spoke in strange language, and my hands were wet with blood.'

For a long time Brynhild was silent. At last she said: 'This dream is the same as the other. The hart from the forest is a great king from a foreign land. He shall be slain at your feet; but be comforted, for you have had the spring of life, and the summer draws near. The daughter of a conquering race would not desire constant peace. You will have joy and sorrow. You may understand the howling wolves, and your right hand may be wet with blood, but rejoice in the love that you have, and in that which shall come. And come again to Lymdale, to bless the friends who love you.'

They drank the parting cup. The Niblung maidens put on their dark blue cloaks, and the golden wains were driven slowly homeward, under the light of the moon.

SIGURD AT LYMDALE

as told by Sarah Powers Bradish

I. HIS ARRIVAL

Heimir, king of Lymdale, whose wife was the sister of Brynhild, had brave sons and fair daughters. He was a valiant king, and often led his warriors in battle, but in time of peace he taught them to cultivate the rich fields of Lymdale, and to look after their sheep and cattle.

One spring morning, King Heimir and his princes and earls were about to mount their horses for the chase, when they saw a warrior approaching. He rode a grey horse, and his armour was all of gold. His fair hair waved in the breeze, and his bright eyes won the hearts of all who looked upon him.

Heimir, putting away his spear, saluted the stranger, whom he begged to stay with his people for a little time, and, offering him the hospitality of his home, asked whence he came.

The horseman answered: 'I am the son of a king, but I alone am left of all my kin. I am of the Völsung race, and they were the sons of Odin.

'I am young, but I have sought wisdom. I have no army, but I, alone, have slain the dragon, and taken his treasure. My name is Sigurd, and I was brought up in the land of the Helper. I am grateful for your welcome, and tonight I will stay in your palace, but tomorrow I must go to Lymdale.'

As Sigurd leaped from the saddle, Heimir said:

'You have already come to Lymdale. I am King Heimir, and am better skilled in the touch of the harp than in the arts of war.'

The princes and earls, who had heard of Sigurd's exploits, looked with admiration on his bright face. They gave up the hunt, and went with him into Heimir's hall, where they spent the day in feasting and song. They talked of the dragon and the Glittering Heath. Four strong men brought in the treasure, and the earls gazed, with ever-increasing wonder, at the shining armour, the cunningly wrought rings and the blocks of gold.

II. SIGURD FINDS BRYNHILD

The next day they went out to hunt. Sigurd was riding alone; the hounds had gone on, and his hawk was sitting on his hand. He was thinking of Brynhild, when he saw a white house among the trees, on the roof of which many doves were sitting in the sun. The hawk flew straight as an arrow toward the house. Sigurd expected to see him attack the doves; but he flew to a window in the tower, and looked within. Then he cried out, as the ravens of Odin cry when they see the morning sun, and flew in at the casement.

'Here is the dwelling of an earl,' thought Sigurd, 'or perhaps of a prince, of whom they have not told me. I will go in to claim my hawk, and find a friend.'

No servant answered his call, so he entered the open door. He saw a staircase, and followed the stairway, which led to a chamber in the tower. His hawk was perched in a window, and on a raised seat sat a beautiful woman, clothed in white, with gold bracelets

SIGURD AT LYMDALE

on her arms. Her embroidery frames stood before her, and in a golden web she was working scenes from the lives of the Völsungs, such as the taking of the sword from the Branstock, the death of Sigmund, Queen Hiordis in the house of the Helper, the beautiful babe named by the Helper and his son, the child in the smithy of the dwarf, the youth taking Greyfell, the forging of the sword, the dragon on his bed of gold, the eagles on the Glittering Heath, the death of the dragon and the dwarf, the journey across the desert, the flaming mountain top, Greyfell and his rider dashing through the fire, the sleeping maiden, forests, meadows, cities and seas, and Sigurd in them all.

With wonder Sigurd saw all this, as he stood in the doorway, and when the woman raised her head, he looked into the eyes of Brynhild. Both were silent. Sigurd was the first to speak, 'Hail, lady and queen! Hail, fairest of the earth!'

Brynhild answered him kindly, as she rose, and led him to a seat beside her. They talked of their separation, and of the joy of meeting again.

Brynhild said:

> 'I bid thee remember the word that I have sworn,
> How the sun shall turn to blackness, and the last day
>   be outworn,
> Ere I forget thee, Sigurd, and the kindness of thy face.'

Sigurd answered:

> 'O Brynhild, remember how I swore,
> That the sun should die in the heavens, and day come
>   back no more,

> Ere I forget thy wisdom, and thine heart of inmost
>   love.'

Then they talked of the days to come, when they should sit on the throne together.

> And they saw their crowned children, and the kindred
>   of the kings,
> And deeds in the world arising, and the day of better
>   things,
> All the earthly exaltation, till their pomp of life should
>   be passed,
> And soft on the bosom of God their love should be
>   laid at the last.

THE WOOING OF BRYNHILD

as told by Sarah Powers Bradish

I. THE OATH OF BROTHERHOOD

Soon after the wedding, Sigurd went to the Doom Ring with Gunnar and Hogni. They cut a piece of turf, and turned it back, so as to leave the earth exposed. With the point of his sword, each opened a vein in his arm; and they let the blood trickle down into the earth. Then they knelt, with their hands upon the spot that had received the blood, and took the oath of brotherhood:

> Each man, at his brother's bidding, to come with the blade in his hand,
> Though the fire and the flood should sunder, and the very gods withstand.
> Each man to love and cherish his brother's hope and will;
> Each man to avenge his brother, when the Norns his fate fulfil.

Sigurd took part in all the work of the kings, and often sat in the Doom Ring, to decide the disputes of the people. The poor were glad to see him there, because he always saw that justice was done; and it is said that the sorrowful loved him best.

II. GRIMHILD URGES GUNNAR TO WED

The old king, Giuki, died; and Gunnar succeeded him on the throne.

One day, Grimhild came to him, and said: 'You have been a good son, a brave warrior and a wise ruler; but the reign of the Niblungs will end with you, unless you take a wife from among the kings' daughters.'

Gunnar answered: 'You are not speaking hastily, mother? You must have found the king's daughter whom you would have me choose.'

Grimhild said: 'In the land of Lymdale is a golden-roofed castle, around which fierce fires burn continually. Within the castle dwells the wisest of maidens, who is as beautiful as she is wise, and as brave as she is beautiful. Yet the sons of the kings pass by, because they are afraid of the flickering flame. She has said that she will wed the man who knows no fear; but he must prove his courage by riding through the circle of fire.'

Then she appealed to Sigurd, to urge Gunnar to win this maiden for his bride. And Sigurd answered that, of all the sons of men, it was most fitting that Gunnar should wed this peerless maiden.

Gunnar said: 'I am contented with my kingdom, and satisfied with the companionship of my brothers; but, in obedience to my mother's wish, I will try to win this princess.'

'Not yet, my son,' said Grimhild; 'we must know the will of the Norns.'

Then Grimhild shut herself up alone, and mixed a magic drink, which she gave to her three sons, to make them do her bidding. She told Gunnar many tales, which made him think of the maiden by day, and dream of her by night.

III. SIGURD WINS BRYNHILD FOR GUNNAR

One morning in May, Gunnar rose early and called his brothers, Sigurd and Hogni, to go with him to seek the maiden. They had put on their armour, and their war steeds were ready, when Grimhild came out to give them her blessing and wish them success. Then they rode away to Lymdale.

Toward evening, they came in sight of the fire; and, as night came on, they rode in silence, with drawn swords in hand. The Wrath of Sigurd sent out red gleams, and the Helmet of Dread shone red as blood, in the light of the fire.

Gunnar rode up to the circle of fire; but his war horse, for the first time, refused to obey his command and, instead of entering the flames, wheeled and carried his rider to the place where the two kings were standing.

Hogni said: 'Take Sigurd's horse.' So Sigurd gave Greyfell to Gunnar, and offered him his armour. But Hogni thought that Gunnar had better keep his own armour.

Gunnar thanked Sigurd; and, springing into the saddle, gathered the reins in his hand; but Greyfell refused to stir. Gunnar cried out in anger that Sigurd was mocking him; but Hogni said, 'Come, Gunnar, stand by Sigurd, take his hand in yours, and look into his face.'

Gunnar took Sigurd's hand, while Hogni repeated his mother's magic words, which made them exchange forms, so that Sigurd looked like Gunnar, and Gunnar looked like Sigurd.

Sigurd, in the shape of Gunnar, leaped into the saddle; and Greyfell bore him safely through the circle of fire, which died away, leaving a ring of white ashes, after the horse and rider had passed.

Sigurd entered the hall, and found Brynhild sitting upon the throne, with a gold crown on her head, and a sword in her hand. Her face was stern and sorrowful; for she had been confident that none but Sigurd would ride through the flickering flame; and now she saw the steel-blue armour and long black hair of the Niblung king.

They gazed at each other in silence until Brynhild said:

'King, King, who art thou that cometh, thou lord of the cloudy gear?'

Sigurd answered, with Gunnar's voice, that he was Gunnar, King of the Niblungs. Then he reminded her of her promise to wed the man who should ride through the fire; and he claimed her as the Queen of the Niblungs.

Brynhild was silent for a time. At last she called him to the high-seat, and said that she would be Gunnar's wife. He drew his sword, and they sat with the naked blade between them while they talked. When it was time for him to go back to the brothers, he gave Brynhild a gold ring; and she drew from her finger the ring of Andvari, and gave it to him, saying, 'It was my dearest treasure.' Sigurd put the ring on his finger; but it brought no memory of the past. He strode out of the hall, mounted Greyfell, and rode away, with downcast eyes.

Hogni spoke to him; and, looking up, he saw a man in golden armour, sitting on a horse. Sigurd did not speak, but stretched out his hand to Gunnar: and they looked into each other's eyes, until the charm of Grimhild's words, uttered by Hogni, changed them into their own forms again. Then Sigurd said to Gunnar, 'Brynhild will be your wife, and will come to the Niblung palace within ten days.'

The three kings returned to the Niblung hall, and told Grimhild how Sigurd had won a bride for Gunnar; and she made a feast in honour of his success. After the feast, Gudrun asked Sigurd how it was that he wore a different ring on his finger. He told her that Brynhild had given it to him, thinking that he was Gunnar; and that Brynhild then had the ring that he was accustomed to wear. Then, with loving words, he took the ring from his finger and put it on Gudrun's.

IV. THE WEDDING OF BRYNHILD AND GUNNAR

Early on the morning of the tenth day, the watchman on the tower called out that many people were coming over the mountains. Then the kings rode out to meet Brynhild and her attendants.

Brynhild rode alone in a golden wagon drawn by snow-white oxen. She sat on a carved-ivory seat, covered with dark blue bench cloths. She saluted the Niblungs, and they rode together to the king's house. When they arrived at the gate, she stood up and blessed the house of Gunnar. The tall war chiefs came out to meet her, and, in the doorway, she saw one in cloudy garments whom she recognized as Gunnar from his ruddy cheeks and long black hair; and she blessed him as the hero of the flickering flame.

Then she received the war duke's greeting; and Gunnar presented his brother, Hogni, but he said that his youngest brother, Guttorm, had gone to the eastern wars; and she asked, 'Who is the fourth king? I thought there were but three.'

Gunnar answered that the fourth king was not of their blood, but that he had been their most welcome guest, and was now their brother, and that his name was Sigurd the Völsung.

She knew the name, but she turned, unmoved, to receive the homage of the Niblung people, and the greeting of Grimhild. Sigurd looked down from the high-seat where he sat by Gudrun's side. Grimhild's spell was broken, and he remembered the sleeping maiden and the words they had spoken on Hindfeirs top.

He led Gudrun down to Brynhild, who greeted him very kindly, though she had no word for Gudrun. The music sounded in the hall; the eagles screamed above the roof; and the wedding feast began.

THE QUARREL OF THE QUEENS

as told by Sarah Powers Bradish

I. THE MORNING BATH

Guttorm returned from the wars, and took his former place in the hearts of the Niblungs, although he had learned to love fighting above all things.

Brynhild was Queen of the Niblungs, and no one guessed that she was unhappy. She often talked with Gudrun, and boasted of her husband, Gunnar, who rode through the fire to win her. But Gudrun said nothing in reply, though she well knew the story of that ride.

Hogni, the wise, grew wiser every day. He alone understood the scheming of his mother, Grimhild; and saw that her feet were going down a path from which they could never return.

Gunnar lived quietly with his wife, though he listened to his mother, who talked constantly of the 'hoard of gold', 'supplanters of kings' and 'leaders of war'. He said it was nothing; but, in the long hours of the night, he turned his mother's words in his mind, and wondered whether Sigurd were a 'supplanter of kings'.

One morning, Brynhild rose early to go to the baths in the river. She had hardly passed the screen of rose and hawthorn, when she saw Gudrun, and bade her go into the water first, because she was the sister of Gunnar.

Gudrun said that a wife was more than a sister, and that if Sigurd's sister were there, she would not give place to her sister-in-law. But, since Sigurd was the greater king, she would accept Brynhild's courtesy; and she stepped into the water.

Brynhild then waded far out into the stream, and Gudrun asked why she went so far away. She replied that they must always be far apart, because she was the wife of a great king, who rode through the flickering flame to win her, while Sigurd stood waiting at the door like a servant; besides, Sigurd was only a vassal of the Helper.

Gudrun waded up the stream to Brynhild; and holding out her hand on which sparkled the ring of Andvari, said, 'You may know by this, whether the greatest of kings and the bravest of men is your husband.'

Brynhild grew white, as she asked, 'By all you love, where did you get that ring?'

Gudrun laughed and said, 'Do you think that my brother Gunnar gave this ring to me?' And then she told Brynhild that Sigurd had given it to her, on his return from Lymdale where, in the form of Gunnar, he had ridden through the flickering flame, and secured her promise to be the wife of Gunnar and the Queen of the Niblungs.

Then Brynhild, pale as death, sprang upon the bank, threw her robe about her, and ran across the fields. But Gudrun came slowly from the water with triumph in her face.

II. GUDRUN'S REPENTANCE

As Gudrun walked home, she remembered that Sigurd had charged her to say nothing about the ride through the flickering flame, or the ring of Andvari; and she was sorry that she had spoken so hastily. In the evening, she went to Brynhild, to ask her to forgive the words spoken in the morning.

Brynhild said that she regretted her own thoughtless words, and that she would forget it all, if Gudrun would only say that her brother Gunnar had given her the ring. But Gudrun said, 'Shall I tell a lie to hide the shame of Gunnar?' and she showed the ring again, and repeated the story she had told in the morning.

Brynhild turned and cursed the house that she had blessed on her wedding day. Then, overcome with chagrin, she lay ill upon her bed. Gunnar came to comfort her, and to beg her to tell him of her trouble.

She said, 'Tell me, Gunnar, that you gave Andvari's ring to Gudrun.'

Gunnar left the room, without speaking.

Gudrun sent her maidens to Brynhild; but they came back, saying they dared not enter her chamber. She sought her brother, Gunnar, whom she found sitting alone, with his drawn sword lying across his knees; and she said: 'O Gunnar, go to her and say that my heart is grieved with her grief, and I mourn for her evil day.' But Gunnar said he could not undo the work of a traitor.

She hastened to Hogni, who sat with his armour on, and his naked sword lying across his knees; and entreated him to convey her message to Brynhild.

But he said: 'I will not go to Brynhild, lest I make the matter worse; there are words that cut deeper than the sharpest sword.

The Norns have ordered, and we must submit.'

Then she found Sigurd wearing his hauberk of gold, and his Helmet of Dread, with his sword lying across his knees. She asked him to go to Brynhild; and he consented.

When he entered the open door of Brynhild's room, she asked why he had deceived her; for she knew nothing about the cup of forgetfulness that Grimhild had given him. They talked a long time, and he tried to comfort her. At last, he offered to put away Gudrun; but she would not consent to that, and he went out. She sent for Gunnar, and asked him to slay Sigurd before the sun rose again.

III. THE DEATH OF SIGURD

Gunnar tore the peace strings from his sword, and went to Grimhild and Hogni. He threw the sword between them, as they were sitting together.

'For whom are the peace strings rent?' asked Grimhild; and he told her that he must take the life of Sigurd. Hogni reminded him of the oath of brotherhood; but Grimhild asked for Guttorm, who was not included in the oath of brotherhood.

As they spoke, Guttorm entered the room. Grimhild rose and gave him a cup which she had prepared. Guttorm drank, and cried, 'Where is the foe?'

His mother gave him the cup again, and he asked for his sword. He drank the third time, and put on the armour that his mother brought.

At dawn, he went to Sigurd's room, but shrank from the glance of Sigurd's eyes; and went back to his brothers with his sword unstained.

He went again, and again the bright eyes of Sigurd drove him back. Then footsteps were heard in the hall, and Brynhild stood among them. The third time Guttorm went to the bed of Sigurd, and this time thrust him through with the sword. Then he turned to go away, but fell dead in the doorway, pierced by the Wrath of Sigurd, which the dying Völsung had hurled at him.

Gudrun cried out in grief and terror, 'Awake, O House of the Niblungs, for slain is Sigurd the King!'

IV. GUDRUN'S MOURNING

The people wept for Sigurd, but Gudrun shed no tears. The women wailed, but Gudrun did not sigh. The earls came to her, and ancient men, great warriors, and sweet singers came to comfort her.

But no tears and no lamenting in Gudrun's heart would strive,
With the deadly chill of sorrow, that none may bear and live.

The daughters of kings and earls told her of their sorrows. Her father's sister said that her king was slain beside her, and then death claimed her sister, all her brothers and both her children; and yet she was living a useful and contented life.

Queen Horberg said that her husband and seven sons fell in one war; her father, mother, and four brothers were lost at sea; and she herself was captured by pirates, and made to serve a robber king.

Then a Niblung maid, named Gullrond, drew away the linen from Sigurd's face, which she turned toward Gudrun. When Gudrun saw it, she bowed her head upon it and wept. Then, with a bitter cry, she left the high-seat and fled from the house.

V. THE DEATH OF BRYNHILD

Brynhild stood by a pillar and gazed long at the wounds of Sigurd. Then she went to her room and lay upon her couch. Gunnar came to her, but could speak no word of cheer.

She bade her maidens bring her finest linen, her best robes, and all her jewels. When they were spread before her, she rose and dressed herself in them. 'Now,' she said, 'bring the sword that I carried when I chose the slain.'

They brought it, and she laid it unsheathed across her knees, and bade the maidens take whatever they might choose from the store of gold and jewels that her father had given her; but the weeping maidens touched none of her gifts. She stood up, and the point of the sword pierced her heart.

They were laying her on the bed when Gunnar entered, and she opened her eyes and asked that she might be laid on Sigurd's funeral pyre with the Wrath of Sigurd between them.

The maidens wept, and Gunnar said:

'Wail on; but, amid your weeping, lay hand to the glorious dead
That not alone, for an hour, may lie Queen Brynhild's head;
For there have been heavy tidings, and the mightiest under shield
Is laid on the bale high builded in the Niblungs' hallowed field.
Fare forth! For he abideth, and we do All-Father wrong,
If the shining Valhal's pavement await their feet o'erlong.'

They carried Brynhild out to the mound on which Sigurd lay with his shield, his hauberk of gold, and Helmet of Dread, and his sword, the Wrath of Sigurd. An old man ascended the pyre, and held the sword unsheathed until Brynhild's body had been placed on the bed that had been prepared for it. Then he laid the sword between them, and the earls applied the torches.

> They are gone: the lovely, the mighty, the hope of the
>   ancient earth!
> It shall labour and bear the burden, as before the day
>   of their birth;
> It shall groan, in its blind abiding, for the day that
>   Sigurd hath sped,
> And the hour that Brynhild hath hastened, and the
>   dawn that waketh the dead;
> It shall yearn and be oft-times holpen, and forget their
>   deeds no more,
> Till the new sun beams on Baldr, and the happy sealess
>   shore.

THE END OF THE TREASURE

as told by Sarah Powers Bradish

When Gudrun fled from the Niblung palace, she went into the forest, where the wolves howled night and day. She did not fear them, for she did not care to live after Sigurd was gone; but they did not hurt her. She went on until she came to a pleasant land, where the people were kind and good. It was the land of the Helper: and King Elf gave her a home in his own house, where she lived with Queen Thora, whom King Elf had married after the death of Hiordis. Gudrun spent the time in teaching the peasant girls to weave and embroider, and herself embroidered many scenes from the life of Sigurd. She never smiled, but was contented; and, as the years passed, became happy in her work.

At the end of seven years, King Atli, Brynhild's brother, sent an earl to the Niblung court, to ask the hand of Gudrun. Atli was old and ugly, but rich and powerful; and Grimhild said that Gudrun must be his wife. 'But', she said to her sons, 'Gudrun will never listen to you; I must go with you; and we must take her a present of gold, to atone for the murder of her husband.' This they could afford to do, since they had kept the golden treasure which Sigurd had taken from the Glittering Heath.

So the two kings and their mother set out on the journey to the land of the Helper, where they found Gudrun in the house of Queen Thora. They told her why they had come; and she said, 'I will not go with you; I will not be King Atli's wife.'

But Grimhild coaxed and flattered, and finally told her how much trouble her wilful daughter had made. Then Gudrun faltered, and, at last, took the cup her mother offered, and drank the wine. It was the cup of forgetfulness; and she forgot everything, except her love for Sigurd; but she said that, if it would please her mother and brothers, she would become King Atli's queen. Then they rode away together; and, soon after, King Atli claimed his bride.

After a few years, a messenger came from Atli, to say that Gudrun longed to see her brothers. He brought a gold ring, tied with wolf's hair, and engraved with runes. Gudrun had written the runes, to warn her brothers of Atli's treachery; but the messenger had changed some of the letters, to make an invitation, instead of a warning, to the Niblung kings. Hogni suspected that something was wrong, because the ring was tied with wolf's hair, and said, 'By this hair Gudrun means to say, 'Atli is a wolf; beware!'"

Hogni's wife, Kostbera, examined the ring, and found that something had been written over the runes to give them a different meaning. She was greatly alarmed, and told her fears to Glaumvor, Gunnar's wife. That night, they both dreamed of flood, fire and destruction; and both waked their husbands, to beg them not to go to Atli's court.

Gunnar thought that these fears were groundless, and after drinking wine at a banquet, he promised that both he and his brother would visit King Atli and their sister. Hogni said that, the royal promise having been given, it would be cowardly to break it; and they began to prepare for the journey. But the next morning, before it was light, Hogni called his wife's two brothers and asked them to help him dispose of the golden treasure, because it had already made trouble enough.

They went to the treasure house, brought out the gold, loaded it upon wagons, and drove to the water's edge. Then they unhitched the oxen, and, putting their shoulders to the wheels, shoved the wagons into a deep place in the river.

That day the Niblung kings started on the journey, from which they never returned; for King Atli put them to death, because they would not tell what had become of the golden treasure, of which nothing now remained except the ring of Andvari, which Gudrun still wore. After the death of her brothers, Gudrun set fire to Atli's palace while he was sleeping; and, rushing to a cliff, threw herself into the sea. So on her finger, the ring of Andvari, the last piece of gold, went back to the water from which it was taken.

> Ye have heard of Sigurd aforetime, how the foes of
>   God he slew;
> How, forth from the darksome desert, the gold of the
>   waters he drew;
> How he wakened Love on the mountain, and wakened
>   Brynhild the Bright;
> And dwelt upon earth for a season, and shone in all
>   men's sight.
> Ye have heard of the Cloudy People, and the dimming
>   of the day,
> And the latter world's confusion, and Sigurd gone
>   away;
> Now ye know the need of the Niblungs, and the end
>   of broken troth,
> All the death of kings and kindred and the sorrow of
>   Odin, the Goth.